The Wrongs of the Religious Right

Reflections on Science, Secularism and Hindutva

MEERA NANDA

Three Essays
COLLECTIVE

First Edition July 2005
Reprinted 2016

ISBN 978-81-88789-30-6

B-957 Palam Vihar, GURGAON (Haryana) 122 017 India
Phone: 0 9868126587, 0 98683 44843
info@threeessays.com Website: www.threeessays.com
Originally Printed at Chaman Offset, New Delhi

For Ravi and Jaya

CONTENTS

INTRODUCTION

The essays collected in the volume were written during the last year, a year full of political ups and downs. The spring of 2004 sprung the surprise election results from India, handing a defeat to the party of Hindu-tva. But the winter brought the chill of the growing Christian-tva in America, when George W. Bush and a Republican Congress were returned to power, largely on the strength of the conservative Christian vote.

For a secular Indian living in America, there was simply no escape from religious politics. Just when you thought you had won at least a temporary respite from religious nationalism in the country of your birth, the religion bug bit the country of your residence. India, Hindu nationalists tell us, is a Hindu country; America, the Christian fundamentalists insist, is a Judeo-Christian country. What are the godless secularists to do? Are they fated to remain a much scapegoated minority everywhere they go? Must all nations define themselves by their Gods?

The November elections in America woke me out of my intellectual complacency about the country that I have called home for many years. While I have always been concerned about America's many flaws, especially its aggressive unilateralism abroad and the ghastly inequities at home, I never doubted the sturdiness of its great wall separating the state from the church. Yes, distinctively Christian symbols and rituals did play a ceremonial role in the affairs of the state. But as long as there were checks and balances against any religion actively intervening in the political processes and policy matters, the civic religion of America was not particularly jarring.

I know now that the wall that Jefferson built has developed gaping holes. The wall obviously did not prevent the conservative Christian churches and lobbies from openly campaigning for Bush and the Republican Party. The two hundred plus years of legal and constitutional precedent have not kept George W. Bush from practically handing over policy matters affecting school curricula, medical research, personal laws regarding marriage and reproduction, and even foreign policy to Christian zealots. It still amazes and shocks me how easily the wall has been breached and how little public outcry there has been when it is becoming harder by the day to distinguish elected officials from church preachers.

The first essay, "Secularism without Secularization?: Reflections on the Religious Right in America and India" was born of the scales-falling-off-my-eyes experience I had during the last American elections. This essay is an exercise in "comparative secularism": it offers a comparative analysis of the historical evolution, strengths and weaknesses of the American "wall of separation" model and the Indian "wheel of law" model of secularism.

Secularism, whatever the model, is only as strong as cultural secularization is deep; no secularism without secularization of the civil society – this is the central thesis that I defend in this essay. Societies where traditional religions with preternatural beliefs still hold sway in personal lives and social relationships can give themselves secular constitutions for any number of political contingencies (e.g., securing religious liberties, as in America, or maintaining communal peace, as in India). But unless there is a gradual diminution of traditional religiosity, and unless the cultural habit of accepting authority based upon faith and/or non-sensory, mystical experiences gives way to a cultural habit of demanding good, falsifiable evidence, secularism will forever remain threatened by those who invoke metaphysical verities backed by God, sacred books and tradition. For all the appearances of hyper-modernity, this larger transformation of cultural habits has not gone as far in America, as it has in Western European countries which experienced a more radical and skeptical confrontation with established religious orders. India has a much longer distance to cover, since it has managed to modernize its infrastructure without any serious challenges to the cultural ideals of Absolute Truth and enchanted nature derived from elite, Brahminical forms of Hinduism.

The other two essays are devoted to exploring the various facets of how the traditional Hindu Weltanschauung sustains itself, even as India modernizes the technologies of production and power. Chapter two, "Hindu Ecology in the Age of Hindutva: Dangers of Religious Environmentalism in India" examines how Hinduism has lately been reinterpreted as an ecological religion, a religion of deep ecology which treats the natural order as sacred. With unintended help from India's environmental movement, defenders of Sanskritic Hinduism have succeeded in reframing India's major ecology movements, especially Chipko, as so many examples of the Hindu reverence for nature as the body of God. This essay also points out the emerging axis of cooperation and unity between the neo-pagan elements of the European New Right and the Hindu nationalists who have welcomed the overtures of the New Right. The same rhetoric of nature's sacredness that has been embraced by some sections of the Indian and Western environmentalist/anti-globalization movements, I caution, also animates the deeply anti-monotheistic, ethnic-religious nationalisms of the New Right. In the atmosphere of growing Islamo-phobia in India and around the world, this neo-pagan, New Right and Hindu nationalist axis can spell a lot of trouble.

The third essay in this volume examines how the postmodern attack on objectivity and universalism of science as covers for power, and the postcolonial demand that India be understood through indigenous conceptual categories inadvertently converge with the celebration of Vedic sciences by Hindu nationalists. This essay extends the thesis I have developed in my previous books, Prophets Facing Backward: Science, Postmodernism and Hindu Nationalism and Breaking the Spell of Dharma.

The point I have tried to drive home in this essay is that secular intellectuals and scientists in India must pay more attention to the scientism of modern Hindu gurus, philosophers and propagandists. By scientism I mean the tendency to conflate the entire corpus of the Vedas with very selectively chosen interpretations of modern physics and biology. Hindu apologists are obviously not alone: all major religions have a tendency to justify their sacred teachings in the language of science and reason. But, what has escaped the notice of secular intellectuals, I argue, is how central this scientism has been to the national chauvinism of neo-Hindu intellectuals. From Dayanand Saraswati, Swami Vivekananda, Sri Aurobindo to the erudite S. Radhakrishnan, neo-Hindus have used the false cover of Hinduism-as-the-religion-of-science-and-reason to assert Hindu superiority over the supposedly irrational, faith-based monotheistic "creeds". Scientism, in other words, has been an essential ingredient of Hindu chauvinism. Moreover, the conflation between Vedic and scientific ontology and epistemology has served to deflect rationalist critiques of popular superstitions which feed all kind of charlatans and frauds who parade as god men and women.

In sum, I have argued that those who defend secularism in India must first defend the distinctiveness of modern science, and that defense of a scientific temper must be given priority. Congress, let us not forget, is the party of soft Hindutva. Secularists simply cannot afford to rest in the afterglow of the last elections, for the arduous task of creating and strengthening a secular culture still lies ahead.

I must acknowledge the kindness of many friends. My special thanks to Ron Herring, Anne Grodzins Gold, Richard Eaton, Stig Toft Madsen,

Steffan Lindberg, Agathe Keller, Gilles Tarabout, Regina Cochrane, David Miller, Laurie Taylor, Latha Menon, Ravi Rajan and Sujata Patel. Meetings with Professor Olivier Herrenschmidt and Harsh Kapoor were most memorable and uplifting. As always, my good friends Alan Sokal and Marin Papa Sokal were wonderful and generous with their time. Many thanks to Asad Zaidi for bringing out the book.

I must also thank the John Templeton Foundation for their research grant that has made it possible for me to devote my time exclusively to research and writing.

The book goes out to Ravi and Jaya, the two most important people in my life. Their love makes it all possible.

SECULARISM WITHOUT SECULARIZATION?

Reflections on the Religious Right in America and India

The question is: Can a social revolution take place before a philosophical revolution has disrupted the authority of traditional values? ... Superstitions cannot be dispelled by legislation. When the leaders of the nation are wedded to hoary traditions, who will make iconoclastic laws? M. N. Roy

History furnishes no example of a priest-ridden people maintaining a free civil government. Thomas Jefferson.

What, I ask, is this thing called infidelity? ...All of us are infidels according to our forefathers' beliefs. Tom Paine.

Introduction

Pat Robertson did something strange shortly after the attacks on the World Trade Center on September 11, 2001: He resigned as the head of the Christian Coalition and with much fanfare, left the position vacant.

Why did Robertson resign? He stepped down to signify that the US president George W. Bush was now the rightful head of the Christian Coalition. The general feeling was that there was no need for Christian activism outside the Oval Office, now that a "man of God" was in charge. As this conservative Christian put it, George Bush "is not the typical politician who 'understands' us, he's one of us."[1]

That was in 2001. Bush's re-election in 2004, which was practically decided by the large turnout by born-again Protestants allied with the most conservative segments of Catholics, has only solidified the already cozy relationship between the Christian Right and the Republican Party.[2] The Christian Right sees George Bush as doing God's work in defeating the Islamic "evil" abroad, and the godless secularist-humanists/feminists/gays at home, a messianism that George Bush himself wears on his sleeve.

There is no denying that there always has been a religious dimension to politics in America. From George Washington and Abraham Lincoln to John Kennedy and Bill Clinton, American presidents have routinely invoked God in their public addresses. But what is new and troubling is the close intermeshing of the Christian conservative think-tanks, lobbyists and preachers with the policy-making apparatus in the White House and the Congress. God and the Bible are no longer serving a merely ceremonial or even an inspirational role: they are being used to direct a deeply socially conservative policy at home and to justify a belligerent foreign policy abroad.[3]

India has already lived through – and reversed, at least for now – the kind of rightwing religious populism that is showing no signs of abating in the United States. George Bush is to the Christian Right what Atal Bihari Vajpayee was to the Hindu nationalists. The Republican Party, in turn, is fast becoming what the BJP has always been to the RSS, namely, the political arm of religious conservatism. The entire ensemble of civil society groups that promote "traditional values" – the Moral Majority, the Christian Coalition, Focus on the Family, to name a few – are to the Republican Party what the VHP, Bajrang Dal, the various swadeshi manchs are to the BJP, namely, the opinion-makers, vote-getters and agitators for the religious right. The preachers and priests who actively engaged in political campaigns from their pulpits, some going to the extent of refusing communion to John Kerry for his support of abortion rights,[4] are no different from the sadhu-sants who rallied for Hindutva causes in countless political "pilgrimages" or yatras. Indeed, Indian politicians can teach George W. Bush a thing or two about his faith-based initiative, for they have a much longer experience in how to dole out public funds to parochial schools and charities without bothering to enforce effective checks against religious instruction, hiring and proselytizing. While the Bush administration is wrangling over how many bricks of new churches can be legally funded through government grants without running afoul of the First Amendment, politicians in India, unencumbered by constitutional prohibitions, have been happily using state coffers to build temples, sponsor pilgrimages and fund parochial schools since the beginning of the Republic. Those who worry about the state of things to come out of faith-based politics in America need look no further than India to know that their worries are justified.

Interestingly, the religious right in both India and the United States came to power by deftly manipulating the rules of electoral democracy. There were no fatwas, no revolutions. Quite the contrary: the victories of the right were accompanied with ever more strident invocations of the virtues of democracy and tolerance, all coded in the language of religiosity and civilizational mission. In his second inaugural address for example, George Bush invoked "freedom" 27 times and "liberty" 12 times, all the time turning them into God's design ("history has a visible direction set by liberty and the author of liberty") with America serving as the agent of this divinely ordained liberty around the world.[5] This soaring paean to freedom hid the dismal reality of lies and deception that led to the war on Iraq and the shameful abuses of prisoners in Abu Gharaib and Guantanamo Bay. The situation is not very different from the soaring rhetoric we heard in India on the "innate tolerance" and "natural secularism" of Hindus even as Hindu mobs were tearing down the Babri masjid and killing Muslim men, women and children in the riots that followed.

Indeed, for all their mutual hostility, Hindu and Christian conser-vatives seem to be following a very similar political script. As his party struggles to regain political momentum, L.K. Advani is beginning to sound very much like an evangelical preacher declaring the BJP to be "the chosen instrument of the Divine" to lead India.[6] And without knowing it, George Bush is taking a leaf out of India's brand of secularism-as- pluralism as he seeks to demolish whatever still remains of the Jeffersonian wall of separation between religion and the state. He is becoming adept at a very Indian-style "equal-respect-for-all religions" rhetoric – inviting a mullah to a prayer session one day and lighting a Diwali lamp in the White House the next – while promoting a born-again agenda through his faith-based initiatives.[7] Now that Hindus in America are at the receiving end of this "equal-respect" strategy, they will hopefully develop a little more respect for the principle of separation of religion and state in India as well.

What is remarkable about the rise of the religious right in India and America – the world's largest and the oldest secular democracies respectively – is how easily the institutions and mechanisms of electoral democracy can be manipulated to yield highly illiberal and distinctively anti-secular governments. In such constitutional democracies, religious fundamentalism and nationalism look more like Orwell's 1984, rather than Taliban's Afgha-nistan, or even the Ayatollahs' Iran. Religious extremism in constitutional democracies will work through doublespeak and not through fatwas.

This essay is devoted to establishing the proposition that until the time constitutional democracies get firmly rooted in a secular culture, they will remain forever vulnerable to the Orwellian manipulation by religious zealots. Without a grounding in secular culture, there is no guarantee that governments, duly chosen by the people, for the people and of the people, will not end up stifling the people in the name of God. No secularization, no secularism – this is the self-evident but often forgotten proposition that this essay seeks to defend.

Godless Constitutions and God-fearing Citizens

On the surface, it may seem quite off the mark to try to understand the rise of the Christian right in America through Indian eyes, or to grapple with issues of secularism and Hindu nationalism in India from the vantage point of what is happening in America today. Why compare apples and oranges, some may wonder. Isn't America, the world's oldest democracy, supposed to be the very prototype of modernity, the culmination of the

Enlightenment, the beacon of religious freedoms and secular polity? And isn't India, the world's largest democracy, still trying to catch up with the technologically developed world, and still mired in tradition and religiosity (which looks like life-transforming spirituality to some, and rank superstition to others)? And, then, isn't there that famous "clash of civilizations"? What could the mostly monistic-polytheistic Hindu India and the largely dualist-monotheistic Protestant America possibly learn from each other?

These differences cannot be denied. And yet, America and India share more than what meets the eye. They share one fundamental contradiction: both are deeply religious societies with secular constitutions. Both societies face a yawning gap between Godless constitutions and god-fearing citizens. While the citizens are literally awash in faith, the states are required by law to remain indifferent to religion altogether (USA) or to any one particular religion (India). As long as this religion-gap between the state and the citizenry continues to widen (rather than shrink, as was anticipated by social theorists), the threat of a religious right take-over of the state through perfectly democratic means will remain. The Republican party in the US might well lose power in the 2008 elections, just as the BJP in India was swept out in 2004. But the underlying cultural dynamic of right-wing populism that brings citizens to vote their religious values and/or identities, often against their material interests, will still remain. As long as ever larger numbers of citizens continue to think that their faith must remain a total way of life, they will continue to see secular states as illegitimate impositions on their right to bring their religion into all aspects of their lives, including electoral politics and public policy regarding education and sexuality.

Both parts of this central contradiction – religiosity of the people and secularity of the state – need a bit of explanation.

Although at very different stages of economic and technological development, America and India share very high levels of popular religiosity. The World Values Survey in 1995 reported an identical and very high proportion – 94 percent – of those surveyed in both countries professing belief in God (Norris and Inglehart, 2004: 90). Other indices of religiosity in America, including participation in religious services (over 50 percent report praying every day, and 40-43 percent report attending church at least once a week), belief in the literal, word-for-word truth of the Bible (40 percent) or belief in the Bible as the Word of God but not literally true (42 percent), afterlife (80 percent), existence of heaven (70 percent), efficacy of prayer (79 percent) are probably closer to levels found in agrarian societies rather than in rest of the industrially advanced Western countries.[8]

This exceptionally high religiosity of Americans – unique among the industrialized countries, except for Ireland and Italy which also show higher rates of religiosity – has been a subject of intense scholarly debates. Many explanations have been offered, including the high influx of immigrants from more religious societies in the Third World, high religious pluralism and greater competition among different religions to attract adherents. But as the careful analysis by Pippa Norris and Ronald Inglehart (2004) shows, neither pluralism nor competition can adequately explain American exceptionalism. What does, however, explain higher religiosity in America as compared to other postindustrial Western societies, is its higher degree of economic inequality and insecurity: cross country data suggest that levels of religiosity show a much closer co-variance with levels of social inequality than with any other factor. Considering America is one of the most unequal of all industrialized societies, with large and growing pockets of insecure and vulnerable populations even among the middle classes, it is not surprising that religion has some extra work to do here – namely, to provide psychological reassurance to face life's insecurities.

Higher degree of popular religiosity does not rule out the possibility that the significance of God and other religious symbols and rituals could be changing. In other words, even though people are praying as often and as sincerely as they used to, God and the church may yet be playing very different roles in their everyday lives than they used to in the past. It has been argued quite plausibly (especially by Steve Bruce, 1996, 2002) that despite high rates of church attendance, most Americans no longer adhere to traditional Christian values when it comes to making personal choices in matters of marriage partners, use of contraception and abortion. Attending church is becoming more a matter of therapy, "positive thinking" and personal choice, rather than obeying God's commandments. Churches often attract adherents by offering precious social services like day-care, addiction and marriage counseling and even dating.[9] But this thinner religiosity, which emphasizes lived experience over church doctrines, is nevertheless contained within the ultimate authority of the Bible, which is often interpreted literally. (Just as in India, where the popular bhakti tradi-tions are held within the authority of the Gita and the Ramayana, with ample references to the Vedas thrown in for good measure.) While the majority of mainline and liberal evangelical churches have learned to accommodate the Bible with modern science, capitalism and multiculturalism of the contemporary American society, the self-described Fundamentalist churches insist upon interpreting the Bible literally. Religion in America may have become "thinner" in substance, less of a way of life and more of a choice, and more eclectic in doctrine than it used to be, but it still constitutes a substantial force for faith, family and (as we shall see) the country as well.

Comparable quantitative data on popular religiosity are hard to come by in India. But by all ethnographic, media and anecdotal accounts, the levels of religiosity are showing no signs of declining, even as modern industry, market economy and urbanization make deeper inroads into the society. Religious books, movies, pilgrimages are growing in popularity, while new temples, yoga ashrams, gurus are all attracting growing numbers of followers. Contemporary religiosity spans the entire range from traditional super-naturalistic beliefs in gods, miracles, horoscopes and the more elite neo-Vedantic and/or New Age practices involving yoga and meditation, combined with beliefs in karma-rebirth and mind-body holism. While India is fast becoming a major player in the global economy, 83 percent of the entire population makes a living in the informal sector, where work and social relations are still largely regulated through customary laws of gender, religion and caste.[10] Religion in this informal sector where most of the India's laboring classes live and work, is still of the "thick" variety as it has not receded from the profane affairs of the society and economy to the extent it has in the more industrialized sectors of the economy.

As in the West, the more educated, urban Indians are finding newer, less caste-driven, more individualistic and eclectic forms of religiosity, with heavy emphases on yoga and spirituality, frequently combined with idol-worship and/or guru-worship.[11] As in America, these new, more experience-oriented, individualized spiritualities are encompassed in a pre-Enlightenment worldview which, in keeping with orthodox Hindu cosmology, affirms the existence of an immortal, conscious vital force or "energy", which is reborn in different bodily forms depending upon the actions in this world. What is unique about these new spiritualities popular among the educated and better off Indians is how this orthodox, vitalistic cosmology, complete with karma and rebirth, is treated as having the sanction of modern science. Whatever little science that does manage to find its way into the temples, ashrams and other religious establishments, gets used up for affirming age-old superstitions. Indeed, the rhetoric of "scientificity" of Hindu sacred texts serves the same function of gaining intellectual acceptance among modern believers, as the claims of literal truth of the Bible serves among Christian fundamentalists, who also invoke the evidence of science to affirm the literal truth of the Genesis story and Noah's flood. The difference of course is that while literalism in America is more of a fringe phenomenon, scoffed at by the more educated and liberal churches, interpreting the Hindu cosmology as "scientifically proven" is an elite phenomenon embraced by the more educated urban middle classes. As in America, religiosity at popular and elite levels tends to be mixed up with strong strains of nationalism, with the landmass of India literally worshipped as a goddess by many devout believers.

These differences notwithstanding, the growing modernization of the economy, industry, legal systems, education in America and India has not eroded the demand for religion to the extent that it has in Western Europe and in parts of East Asia.

This high degree of the persistence of popular religiosity becomes all the more remarkable if one views it against the backdrop of the official policy of secularism. Officially, the states in both countries are constitution-ally obliged to remain neutral regarding matters of faith, while promising all citizens, regardless of their religious affiliation, complete freedom of conscience and the right to practice and propagate their religious beliefs.

America is often held up as a model of a secular state for the rest of the world.[12] The Jeffersonian "wall of separation", prohibiting the state from making any laws either promoting or prohibiting the free exercise of religion, is an integral part of American self-image as a secular and tolerant society.

But what is less well known in America, at least outside the circle of India-watchers, is that India provides a competing model of secularism which also promises complete freedom of religion and conscience to all citizens, but does that without erecting a wall of separation. As has been pointed out by Gary Jacobsohn (2003), the apt metaphor for the Indian variant of secularism is not a wall but a wheel, the wheel of the Law, or the dharma chakra that appears on the national flag: just as the spokes of the wheel must be of equal length, so must all religions be treated with equal respect by the state. The state in India is committed to neutrality not by keeping its hands off religion, nor by keeping religion out of the matters of the state, but by not playing favorites. The Indian Constitution allows the state to intervene in religious laws regulating social and personal relations, and it allows the state to subsidize religious schools and institutions as long as it remains neutral and does not try to reform and/or promote one faith over any other. Under the current Bush administration, America seems to be moving closer to the Indian model. Bush's faith-based initiatives, for example, allow tax-dollars to support the religious aspects of religious charities and non-profit organizations, as long as all faiths have an equal opportunity (at least in theory) to apply for state funds.

Regardless of the model, the conventional wisdom among social scientists has been that a secular state can emerge and thrive even in deeply religious societies. A secular state, we have been told, should not be confused with secularization of the civil society, which implies a decline of religion both in society and in the minds of individuals. According to a much-cited definition by Donald E. Smith (1998[1963]:178), a state is considered secular as long as it "guarantees individual and corporate freedoms of religion, deals with the individual as a citizen irrespective of his religion, is not constitu-tionally connected to a particular religion, nor seeks either to promote or interfere with religion." As long as a state is constitutionally committed to these ideals, and has legal and political safeguards to enforce them, it is technically a secular state. Religiosity of the citizens, as long as it is kept limited to their private lives, is taken to be irrelevant to the function-ing of such a state.[13] Indeed, the American experience of a functioning secular state and un-secular society has been held up as a counter to the argument that a sustainable secular state requires a secularization of the life-world of citizens.[14]

This essay will question this conventional wisdom by demonstrating the fragility of secularism as a constitutional imperative in the absence of secularization of consciousness and culture. I will argue that the religionization of politics, expressed in fundamentalist and/or nationalist movements, will remain a potential threat in officially secular, liberal democratic societies where traditional religions continue to serve as the dominant sources of social values and social-political identities. Liberal democracies thrive best in an atmosphere of low intensity of religious beliefs in the civil society. Without a wall of separation going up in the consciousness of the citizens between what belongs to god and what to each other and to nature, there can be no wall of separation between the state and religion. Secular laws must be anchored in a secular worldview;

otherwise they will continue to be breached by those who want their religion "strong", whole and public. M.N. Roy (1968), the great radical humanist had this to say when India adopted a secular constitution in 1950: "secularism is not a political institution; it is a cultural atmosphere which cannot be created by the proclamation of individuals, however highly placed and intensely sincere."

The rest of this essay will concern itself with defending the priority of secularization over secularism. I will examine three scenarios:

1. Secular states, religious citizens. Here I will examine the historical genesis of this gap. The internal divisions within Protestant sects in America regarding the appropriateness of separation of church and state will hopefully lay to rest the myth, widespread among many Indian intellectuals that "secularism is a gift of Christianity", and therefore culturally incompa-tible with the native genius of Hindus. On the other hand, Americans, as they appear ever more ready to allow religion into the institutions of the state, can learn cautionary lessons from India's model of secularism which does not prohibit the state from intervening in religious matters.

2. Religious citizens, religious nations. Here I will examine the possibility that other things being roughly equal, societies with more widespread and intense religiosity will be more prone to religious political movements with nationalistic overtones, or as Samuel Huntington (2004) has put it, "countries that are more religious tend to be more nationalistic". I will argue that both America and India show a close intermeshing of God or the Goddess (as in India) and country. The cult of the nation has a distinctively messianic, self-universalizing dimension in both countries. Americans tend to see their country as God's Chosen Country, with a mission to spread the light of liberty around the world. Indians, especially the more ideologically articulate among them, tend to see India as a uniquely "spiritual" country, as the land of perennial wisdom, whose mission is to save the entire world by spiritualizing the forces of modernity unleashed by Western materialism. Religiosity, I will argue here, is not just a matter of personal faith and consolation. Rather, religiosity is the medium through which nations can define their identities.

3. Secular culture for secular societies. This thesis will argue for a new Enlightenment that respects the legitimate rights of conscience and freedom of religion, acknowledges the place of religion in the public sphere, but denies it any special claim on morality, social values or knowledge.

Contrary to the predictions, it is clear that neither religion, nor the nation-states are going to wither away soon. It is also clear that an absolute separation of religion and the state is neither possible (for religious sensibilities do set the background rhythms and tone of a society), nor even desirable (for religions can serve as a check on the state violations of human dignity). Because they continue to be so vital and fundamental even in modern societies, religious doctrines, practices and institutions require far more critical engagement than any other element of cultural life. Thus, the urgent need for renewing the Enlightenment.

The New Enlightenment, as I see it, would mean a renewed critical engagement with the content of religious cosmology and the seemingly factual basis of its claims to authority. In practice this would mean that any empirical claims that follow from religious prescriptions in public policy will have to pass the tests of rigorous, impartial scientific tests. Assertions of sacredness and tradition can claim no automatic authority if they are derived from already falsified and/or un-falsifiable dogmas. Rather than try to recover the "good" aspects of faith against the "bad" parts, as some in the religious left tend to do, I will argue that we should accept nothing on faith, and learn to evaluate values by examining their empirical consequences. Creation of a secular culture and secular values, which do not depend upon anything external to collective human experience – neither God, nor natural order and no red books either – is the best defense of a secular state. It is a difficult course of action: there are no security blankets to hold on to. But it is the only course of action open to human beings if they are not to destroy themselves in the name of their gods, be these gods of religion or the gods of progress-at-all-costs.

The Genesis of Secular Constitutions in America and India

The creation of secular states in India and the United States was revolutionary because it marked a break from the past – from the state-controlled Church of England in America, and the institution of caste in India. But in both cases, this revolutionary innovation in politics was not accompanied by a corresponding revolution in beliefs: the emergence of secular states did not lessen the cultural authority of conventional religions based upon belief in the supernatural. On the contrary, in both countries, this revolutionary break with the past was justified in a largely religious vocabulary, and absorbed into the traditional religious weltanschauung.

There are serious Indian scholars of religion, notably the eminent sociologist T.N. Madan, who argue that Christianity being a dualistic religion (that is, a faith that separates a transcendent God from nature and from the affairs of here-and-now) is innately more conducive to a secular state. The lesson they draw from this observation is that the very idea of secularism as separation of church and state is a Christian idea, not well-suited for the largely Hindu India where the secular affairs of this world are encompassed by concerns for spiritual salvation (Madan, 1989). And then there are those ideologues of the Hindu right, notably, Sita Ram Goel (2000) and N.S. Rajaram (1995), who claim that only Christianity needed to be secularized because of its long history of theocracy, intolerance and superstitions. A state guided by Hindu culture, they claim, will be "naturally" respectful of difference and conducive to rational thought. Since Hinduism, on their reading, is not a religion but a pluralistic and rational "way of life", the Indian state can only be truly secular if it embraces Hinduism.

How fallacious these anti-secularist arguments are becomes evident when one examines the religious background of the American Revolution which led to the disestablishment of the church. Contrary to those who think that secularism is a Protestant idea, America, a country settled by Protestants, was not born secular: the idea of separation of church from the state had to be struggled for. Christianity does have elements of individual equality and separation of civil government from the Church, but they were politically quite powerless until the time they joined forces with secular ideas of the Enlightenment. And contrary to the anti-Christian rhetoric of Hindutva ideologues, far from being enforcers of theocracy, churches were the major resources for democratization and modernization of the American society. It is true that evangelical churches encouraged a pietistic religion of the heart which often disparaged rationalist ideas – but then, the record of Hindu gurus, priests, astrologers and the countless other assorted charlatans is hardly any better on this account.

Neither the Anglicans who settled the Virginia colony, nor the Puritans who settled the Massachusetts Bay had even the remotest notion of separation of church from the rest of the society. The ruling paradigm was that of a Christian Commonwealth which saw society in a covenant relationship with God: as long people obeyed God's laws, they would enjoy His blessings. As was the case in all pre-modern societies, the state, society, nature and the Church formed a totality. In this totality, the state and the society were expected to obey the same set of laws – the laws of God. (The crucial difference from the traditional Hindu conception of an ideal commonwealth, Ram Rajya, was of course that the laws of God were the same for all who had a covenant relation with God.) The Puritans who established the Massachusetts Bay colony had taken some steps toward separation of politics from the church, ensuring that the ministers of the church could not run for political office (unlike the Archbishops of the Church of England who had enormous political power). But in actual practice, the ministers of the church routinely called upon the power of the civic magistrates to enforce Christian morality, and collect taxes for the state-recognized church. The separation of powers was formal, not substantive.

There was, however, a minority tradition of a more radical separation between church and the state among the more "fundamentalist" Puritan sects, the Baptists (the radical forerunners of today's largely conservative evangelical Southern Baptist Convention) and the Anabaptists (the Amish and the Mennonites). These dissidents challenged the mainstream Puritans' readiness to call upon the power of the state to enforce the dominance of the established churches. Being ultra-pure in their Protestant beliefs, they saw spiritual redemption as purely a matter of individual's relationship with God, and no concern of the state. Unlike today's Christian fundamentalists who proclaim America to be Christian nation, their "fundamentalist" Baptist forefathers vehemently denied that Christianity had anything to do with the country or its government. In their view, "government was the business of men, and church was the business of God. For a magistrate to presume to protect the true religion was to usurp the place of God" (Kramnick and Moore, 1997: 57). God, in other words, was too great and too powerful to need the help of government. It is not that these ultra-Puritans denied that those who run the government should be virtuous (by the lights of Christian teachings, of course), but they denied that the government could ever claim to act on God's behalf. There was always a temptation even among the Baptists to ask Congress to promote Christian morality (e.g., in enforcing Sabbath laws, enforcing temperance and such), but this temptation was held in check by a fervent theological belief in the separation of spheres.[15] It was this "left wing" of Puritanism that made common cause with the Enlightenment rationalism of the Founding Fathers. But as we shall see, this collaboration was based more upon a theological understanding of separation of god and politics, and it was not hospitable to the deist and empiricist worldview of Thomas Jefferson, James Madison and Thomas Paine. In fact, the Baptists and other radicals who supported the wall of separation continued to heartily denounce Jefferson and Paine as "infidels" who were bringing the evils of the French Revolution to the shores of America!

The Christian Commonwealth of the Puritans and the Wall of Separation of the Baptist dissenters represent the split soul of American

Protestantism: the first inclined toward totality and community, and the other toward separation and individualism; the first not reluctant to use state power to do God's work, the other who views it as blasphemy. The commonplace idea in India that protestant Christianity is either innately secularizing or innately theocratic represents the worst kind of essentialist thinking, for it ignores the play of politics and material interests in development of ideas. The difference between the American and Indian experience of secularism does not lie in the "innate" traits of religion, but on the outcome of social and political struggles, underpinned by religious ideals, but never decided by religion alone. In America the minority Puritan traditions of individualism won out, converged partially with secular-liberal philosophies, and became the dominant strain in politics, economy and religion, all at the same time. In India, on the other hand, the minority tradition of equality did win over the ideology of a caste society in the political realm, but could never break free from the dominant religious-cultural ideals of the Hindu commonwealth ("Ram Rajya") and hierarchical inclusivism. (More on the Indian case later in this section).

To continue with the American saga of secularism, the radical puritan sects – Baptists and Anabaptists – made up the "left wing" of the Reformation and had been persecuted by the Anglican Church in England. They were not much liked by the mainstream of Puritan churches in America either, for they were considered too radical and too anti-establishment. But between the founding of America and the American Revolution, Baptists, Methodists and other small sects had spearheaded two Great Awakenings which proved crucial for the disestablishment of the church.

The Great Awakenings were mass revivals in which charismatic traveling preachers, often from the working classes and slaves in the South, without any training in the East Coast universities and seminaries, set out to – literally – spread the gospel. These revivals preached an emotionally charged Christianity in which what counted was spiritual transformation through a direct experience of Christ, the experience of being "born again". This evangelical form of Christianity was instrumental in spreading a democratic and egalitarian, but at the same time, an anti-intellectual form of religious faith which often combined direct experience of being born again with the literal truth of the Bible. As Richard Hofstadter shows in his 1962 classic, Anti-Intellectualism in American Life, this form of Christianity spread widely because it was more conducive to the anti-authoritarian, anti-aristocratic, anti-East Coast sensibilities of the populations settling the newer, westward colonies. The slave population in the south responded especially well to the Baptist and Methodist revivals as they gave them an opportunity to establish their own churches, led by their own lay preachers. The revivals changed the religious geography of the country: by the end of the eighteenth century, Baptists and Methodists far outnumbered the Puritans and the Anglicans. Each of the denominations, furthermore, was split into many different churches. The original uniformity had given way to an enormous plurality within the protestant church itself.

It is these Baptists and Methodists who put their support behind the disestablishment clause of the Constitution. While they detested the rationalist and deist Christianity of Thomas Jefferson and openly condemned Thomas Paine as an atheist, they nevertheless helped to ratify the Constitution which barred a religious test for office holders (Article 6 of the US Constitution) and prohibited the state from any direct interference and/or promotion of religion (the First Amendment of the Bill of Rights). They favored disestablishment in part out of their theological belief that it was blasphemous for the state to do God's work (see above), and partly out of a fear of persecution from a church backed by state power. Whereas Jefferson, Madison, Paine and other more secularist founders were more concerned with the corrupting influences of faith on politics, their evangelical supporters were more worried about the power of the state to regulate their religion. They saw religion as a purely private matter which needed to be protected from the corrupting influences of politics.

This purely strategic alliance of ideological opposites – the freethinkers among the founding fathers and deeply devout evangelical Christians – reflects the divided soul of American religion between rationalism and pietism, and between a modernist impulse and fundamentalist impulse. Contrary to the Hindu right wing portrayal of Christianity as nothing but an irrational and superstitious "creed" (as compared to the rational and eternal natural law of Hinduism), it was the mainline protestant churches in America, along with secular public intellectuals, who kept the rationalist, modernist impulse of the freethinkers alive. As Susan Jacoby concludes in her recent book, Freethinkers, many of the Puritan-founded Congregation-alist churches turned into more liberal and rationalist Unitarian Universalist fellowships which "moved religion itself into the camp of Enlightenment rationalism" (p. 52). The modernist impulse in American Protestantism, according to William Hutchinson, a historian of American religion, represented a genuine embrace of scientific worldview which "made modern science its criterion and then, as an afterthought, tried to retain what [could be retained] of the Christian tradition," Hutchinson, 1976: 7). In other words, liberal churches accepted that in case of a genuine conflict between science and theology, theology must be reinterpreted and revised. While the more conservative fundamentalist churches continued to read science as evidence of the literal truth of the Bible, mainline churches were more open to rational re-interpretations of the Bible.

In matters of science, this modernist spirit expressed itself not as an outright rejection of God and the Bible, but as wider spread of Jeffersonian deism, which made God more and more distant from the affairs of nature. As George Marsden (1991: 130) points out, by the end of the 18th century, "even many of those who were theologically orthodox adopted a worldview that, in effect had Deist tendencies. They viewed the universe as a machine run by natural laws, and in practice distanced the creator from their understandings of the everyday operations of creation." In other words, a mechanistic philosophy of nature – which is the key to disenchantment of nature – was fully acceptable to even the theologically orthodox Protestants, as long as it left room for the Creator God as the ultimate, albeit distant and methodologically irrelevant, source of natural laws. The period after the Civil War to the end of the First World War (roughly 1865 to 1930) was considered the golden age of secularization and liberalization of Christianity. This was the Gilded Age when America underwent large scale industriali-zation and urbanization. And it was also when Charles Darwin published his Origin of Species (1859). Unlike those pushing for equal time for "creation science" in school curricula today, the vast majority of mainline churches learned to accommodate the most dangerous element of Darwin's theory – namely, evolution through natural selection and without any purpose or goal – with a belief that natural selection was the mechanism by which God chose to act in the physical world. It is true that the modernist impulse in America developed not in a radical confrontation with the Church doctrines (as in France), but in a moderate accommodation between Christian doctrines and the new sciences. But underneath the appearance of "synthesis" and "accord" what was being accepted was a fully naturalistic understanding of nature without any significant reference to God. Mainstream science was being accepted in its entirety, without trying to defend a uniquely Christian faith-based way of knowing, and without trying to put a religious spin on it. The watchmaker God only got a ceremonial bow, while scientific accounts of natural laws were accepted.

Apart from the accommodation of Darwinism, there was also an attempt by well-known neo-orthodox theologians to find new basis for faith which did not bring it in conflict with new developments in science and historical research. They interpreted the supernatural elements in the Bible as poetry or as imaginative allegories not to be accepted literally. In this endeavor, modernism within the churches was supported by important public intellectuals and philosophers in the nineteenth century who, in the wake of Darwin, had embraced a pragmatic form of scientific naturalism. Highly regarded public intellectuals like John Dewey, George Santayna, John Herman Randall and Robert Ingersoll tried to popularize a new conception of knowledge that substituted the metaphysical absolutes of received traditions with an empirically adequate, albeit uncertain and forever changing conception of truth.[16] The modernist strands of theology and philosophy, in turn, got aligned with the Social Gospel of the progressive era which tried to play down the other-worldly aspects of salvation in favor of social reform.

But one has to accept the uncomfortable fact that these modernist tendencies remained limited to relatively high-brow churches which tend to attract the better-educated and liberal segments of the society. The secularist-modernist ideas have failed to percolate down into the wider population, which has remained loyal to a less cerebral and often distinctively anti-intellectual forms of evangelical worship. (As the data in the next section will show, evangelical churches have been growing at the expense of more rationalist mainline churches).

In fact, the ascendance of the anti-modernist, conservative Christianity that we are witnessing today is a backlash against the modernism of liberal churches and universities. Christian fundamentalists, as George Marsden (1991:1) aptly describes them, are "evangelicals who are angry" and willing to fight for what they consider the fundamentals of their faith. They are angry about the thinning of their faith under the impact of secular ideas, the challenge to the supernatural and the loss of hegemony of the "original" white Protestant Americans over the dominant culture. After a period of withdrawal from political life following the famous Scopes trial in 1925,[17] conservative Christians re-emerged in the 1980s to actively campaign for Ronald Reagan. They were mobilized to battle secularist institutions on matters regarding school prayer, abortion, equal time for creation science/intelligent design and more recently, the right to display the Ten Commandments in public places. The 9/11 attacks have given them a new cause – defense of the "homeland" against Islamic "evil".

Today's fundamentalists represent a throwback to the more conser-vative "Christian commonwealth" tradition of Puritanism that does not hesitate in using state power to enforce religious correctness. The presidency of George W. Bush is aiding and abetting these conservative tendencies.

As in the American case, the evolution of a secular state in India bears the marks of the conflicts between the secular humanism of Nehru, Ambedkar and other founding fathers of the Indian Republic, and the integral humanism of Gandhi and other neo-Hindu nationalists.

The essential difference with the American experience, of course, is that the Indian Constitution has no such thing as the First Amendment prohibition on the state from enacting any law that either establishes religion or prohibits its free expression. Instead of the American-style "negative secularism", the Indian model calls for "positive secularism" which allows the state to both censor and promote religion. It is not a wall of separation that qualifies India as a secular state but rather what Jacobsohn (2003) has called the "wheel of law", which symbolizes the idea of sarva dharma sambhava, or "equal respect for all religions". The idea is that just as a wheel moves because all the spokes are of equal length, the Indian state will be even-handed and impartial as it interferes with and/or promotes different religious faiths of the people of India.

Another way to understand the Indian model of secularism is to refer to Donald Smith's definition of secular state quoted above. According to this definition, a state is secular if it meets four conditions:

a. guarantees individual and corporate freedoms of religion;
b. deals with the individual as a citizen irrespective of his religion;
c. is not constitutionally connected to a particular religion; and finally,
d. does not seek either to promote or interfere with religion.

The Indian Constitution promises to safeguard the first three conditions not by prohibiting the state from d. but by demanding that the state promotes or interferes with all religions equally, without adopting any religion as the religion of the state.

It is this promise of equal treatment of all religions – the doctrine of sarva dharma samabhava – that is the core of the Indian model of "positive secularism".

The "positive secularism" of the Indian state was born of the twin necessities of creating a democratic state and ensuring peace between Hindus, Muslims and other minorities after the terrible bloodletting of partition. The crowning achievement of the new Indian state was not the distancing of the state from religion. It was rather the commitment to the creation of a democratic society in which all citizens were formally equal before the law, regardless of their caste, class, gender and religious faith. If religious liberty was the principle on which the secular-minded Jeffersonians and the theologically-conservative Baptists could agree in America, the need for a democratic society without the divisions of caste was the unifying ground between the secular-humanists like Nehru, Ambedkar and other members of the socialist wing of the Congress, and the more traditionalist leaders influenced by neo-Hindu revival. Many of the heroes of this revivalist wing of the Congress – figures like Sardar Patel, Bal Gangadhar Tilak, Lajpat Rai, S. Radhakrishnan and Sri Aurbindo – are revered among contemporary Hindu nationalists.

This commitment to the creation of a democratic state – which is fundamentally anti-caste[18] – in a society with a long history of caste hierarchies required, above all, the disestablishment of caste. Since the institution of caste has cosmological and customary justifications in Hinduism, the constitutional disestablishment of caste required a reform of Hinduism. Apart from caste, there were many cruel and inegalitarian customs in all faiths which had the blessings of religion, such as purdah, polygamy (among both Muslims and Hindus), child marriage, dowry, dedication of girls to Gods, to name just a few.

Being a charter for social reform, the Indian Constitution did not have the luxury to remain indifferent to the many social ills which had the blessings of the many religions of India. Neither did the state have the luxury to leave religious reform to religious bodies, since Hinduism and Islam simply do not have organized ecclesiastical institutions that could be called upon to take the responsibility. How to reform religion without stifling the freedom of religion of people of diverse faiths was the daunting challenge facing the framers of the Indian Constitution. That India did not take the easy way out and simply ban all religious expression (as was attempted in the Soviet model of secularism), or demand reform through official decrees (as in Turkey and Iran) does the country proud. But the solution it did work out – namely, state neutrality toward all religions – created its own set of problems, chief among them being a serious neglect of secularization of the civil society.

The Indian Constitution walks the fine line between protecting religious freedom while giving the state and the courts the right to censor those secular aspects of religious practices which clash with the fundamental right of equal citizenship. Thus Article 25 of the Constitution allows "all persons…freedom of conscience and the right freely to profess, practice and propagate" their religious beliefs, except when the secular aspects of religious practices conflict with other fundamental rights. While this compromise appears quite sound in principle, in practice it opened the door to judicial activism, allowing judges to interpret what is properly religious and therefore protected by law, and what are the secular aspects of religion which can be legislated in the interest of equality. Other provisions in the Constitution give all religious faiths equal rights to establish institutions in order to collectively practice and propagate their faith. What is more, the Constitution allows for state subsidies for religious institutions, as long as they are not aimed at establishment of an official state religion, but are available for all religions equally. Thus, Article 27 bars use of tax money for benefit of any particular religion, but not for the benefit of all religions. In other words, while there is no compulsion to support an official religion, public funds for religion per se are not prohibited. A very similar law applies to state support of parochial schools: Article 28 stipulates that religious schools can teach religion and still receive state grants as long as they do not compel students to take part in religious instruction.[19]

In all of these crucial areas of state-religion relationship, there is not even a hint of a separation. The Indian state remained deeply engaged in religion, both adopting its celebratory aspects for state functions and reserving the right to reinterpret and reform religious traditions. Under these circumstances, the entire burden of preserving religious freedoms has fallen on the promise that the state and the courts will intervene in and/or celebrate all religions equally, without playing favorites – the famous wheel of dharma which is supposed to have the sanction of long tradition of tolerance in Hinduism.

This model has worked in a fashion. Regardless of the agitation by the Hindu right, the Indian state has not adopted Hinduism as the official religion. And regardless of the many inherent problems of interpretation, Indian courts have tried to balance the imperative for religious reform with a respect for the freedom of religion.

But, clearly, this model has serious drawbacks as well. Above all, allowing the state to intervene in religious affairs has turned religion into one more object of state patronage and political machinations. Professions of even-handedness notwithstanding, it is a fact that the state has refrained from intervening in the Islamic law – giving a good excuse to the Hindu right to incite popular anger against the Muslims and against the secular state. On the other hand, for all the pious professions of neutrality, Hinduism has served as the de facto civil religion of the state – giving religious minorities good reasons to be suspicious of the secular credentials of the state. To top it, the lip service to promotion of a secular outlook through the propagation of a "scientific temper" among the people has invited the wrath of the anti-secularists who see a secular outlook as Western imposition. A large body of literature already exists on the many strengths and weaknesses of the Indian model of secularism.[20]

I don't intend to add to this already vast body of literature. My interest in this essay is different. I want to understand how the state in such intensely religious societies as America and India came to adopt a stance of neutrality toward religion, either through a negative prohibition on state involvement (as in America) or through a positive injunction for fairness and neutrality in state involvement (as in India). I believe that the compromises that went into crafting secular states without a prior (or simultaneous) creation of secular cultures have created the conditions which are conducive to a right wing religious populism. At a minimum, the gap between the secular state and religious populations is creating conditions where religious majorities have come to see themselves as oppressed minorities, at the mercy of a "secular elite" who supposedly run the state and the judiciary. Moreover, when a majority of citizens derive their sense of right and wrong and even – increasingly – the sense of their national identity from their religion, no constitution can really keep politics out of religion and religion out of politics.

As we saw above, evangelical Christians in America gave their support to the Jeffersonian wall of separation for purely political purposes of securing their own religious liberty, even though they openly despised the rationalist, Enlightenment outlook of the Jeffersonians which took a skeptical stance toward church dogmas. A similar alliance of ideological opponents emerged between the secularist and neo-Hindu traditionalists in the Indian National Congress at the time of India's independence. Through the 19th century when the political awakening began in India, up to Independence in 1947 and the adoption of the Constitution in 1950, there had been a growth of a Hindu revivalist sentiment among reformers and modernizers that had edged out the more rationalist, secular critics of Hinduism. Indeed, as Charles Heimsath demonstrated in his well-regarded book, Indian Nationalism and Hindu Social Reform, "Indian nationalism had in fact become, by the first decade of the 20th century, Hindu nationalism for the Hindu leaders of the movement" (p.312). Heimsath's description of the Hindu basis of nationalism is worth quoting in full:

> "... in the development of the reform movement, a third stage emerged during the latter part of the one-hundred period ending with the First World War. Corporate social values suited to national society began to take precedence... and...Hindu society, not a transplanted Western society, was recognized as the proper vehicle for individual self-realization. An intellectual development was beginning in which social reform began to mean a regeneration of the traditional spirit of the nation – a regeneration, political as well as social

> which was founded on religious revival. By the end of the third stage, criticism of the society [came to be based] on the failure of national social life to realize its own innate potentialities, and not on its inferior performance in comparison to Western societies." (Heimsath, 1964:8, emphasis added).

In other words, a regeneration of the supposedly eternal and benevolent spirit of Hinduism, purified of its corruptions, came to be seen as the source of the future development and salvation of modern India. Many of India's best known leaders, including Gandhi and many of the heroes of the contemporary Hindu nationalists, especially Savarkar, Swami Vivekananda, Sri Aurobindo, Sardar Patel, Bal Gangadhar Tilak come from this tradition of Hindu revivalism. Their revivalism was a case of collective amnesia: its version of the past assumed that Hinduism itself – even the supposedly "purified" and "Aryan" versions – had played no role in creating, sustaining and preserving the many social ills of India. India's model of "positive secularism" evolved out of this Hindu revival that edged out secularists like Jawaharlal Nehru, Bhimrao Ambedkar and their many sympathizers among socialists, dalits and religious minorities who wanted a cultural transformation to take precedence over the merely political reform.

Now, "Hindu revival" has never been a Taliban-like movement intent on shutting off the society from modern ideas in order to re-create the original faith-based society. Hindu revivalism is more appropriately described as reactionary modernism in which modern ideas, born of a critique of the sacred cosmopolis, are divested of their Enlightenment and rationalist roots and re-conceptualized and justified in religious and nativist terms: only the words are modern, their meanings are mired in tradition and obscurantism.

The Hindu revivalists were sufficiently impressed by the West to accept the importance of modern ideas like democracy, the need to remove the injustices of untouchability (though not the original four-fold varna), emancipation of women, modern industry and, last but not the least, modern science. But rather than create a new culture that could genuinely support these ideals while taking along rationalized elements of Hindu traditions, Hindu revivalists sought to justify them by invoking ancient scriptural justifications. Becoming modern then became a matter of restoring Hinduism to its pristine spiritualist glory and infusing Indian society with the spirit of this revitalized Hinduism. The only problem with this warm and fuzzy revivalism is that the kind of "secularism" and "science" that the Vedic sources and social customs actually support bear no resemblance with secularism and science as they are understood in the modern, post-Enlightenment world today. What we get is a secularism seeped in religiosity, and science that supports the soul-stuff that underlies all the occultist superstitions of the New Age.

But let me continue with the story of the evolution of secularism in India. While the Indian Constitution was presented to Indians and to the rest of the world as a charter for a modern and secular society, it was in fact understood to be secular in a fundamentally Hindu way. If anything, the brand new Constitution reinstated the brand new, supposedly secular state as a patron of all faiths, which posed no challenge to the social power of the Brahmins. The secular world-outlook of the Indian Jeffersonians – Nehru and Ambedkar, two of the most prominent proponents of cultural transformation and secularization – never received more than an honorable mention as a non-enforceable duty of the state to promote a "scientific temper". M.N. Roy (1948), the Communist turned radical humanist, was not too off the mark when he called the profession of secularism by Hindu traditionalists as "moonshine".

Given that those with socialist-rationalist sympathies and those with Hindu traditionalist sympathies agreed on the need for disestablishment of caste as a precondition for establishment of a democracy, the strict separation of state from religion was never on the agenda. The consensus position that quickly emerged in the Constituent Assembly, without much debate on the meaning of secularism, favored the idea of sarva dharma samabhav. This allowed room for state intervention in the interest of social justice and reform, but at the same time allowed the freedom to practice one's faith. It remains debatable whether the state should have interjected itself in matters of religious reform at all, or left it to India's many faiths to reform themselves through their own devices. Clearly, playing politics with the reform of Muslim personal law, especially in the Shah Bano case, has poured fuel on the Hindu nationalists' complaints of a "pseudo-secular" state overly eager to interfere with Hindu customs, but too timid when it comes to Islamic law. But at the time of India's founding as a republic, this "ameliorative model" of secularism which made room for state intervention in the interest of social equality and in the interest of creating a nation out of diverse faiths had wide support among those who drafted the Constitution.[21]

Like the conservative evangelicals in America who accepted a one-sided wall of separation assuming they were protecting the garden of the church from the wilderness of the state,[22] most of the Indian lawmakers understood secularism as affirming the glory of Hinduism. Secularism, Indian-style, did not demand or encourage any change in the belief systems of the politicians or the public. There were important legal battles over opening Hindu temples to untouchables, polygamy, the right to excommuni-cate, the issue of cow protection and conversions. But on a day to day basis, secularism did not change anything. You were free to wallow in the worst obscurantism, and still call yourself a secularist as long as you were an equal-opportunity obscurantist and paid obeisance to religious dogmas of all faiths! The sight of politicians indulging in conspicuous religiosity – Indira Gandhi was a master of this – and using public money for the support of religious enterprises such as pilgrimages, charities and schools has remained a constant feature of Indian politics from the very beginning. Any principled attempt to keep the state above and beyond matters of faith died with Nehru in 1965. Since then, the state has made only the feeblest attempts to create a new secular outlook through its patronage of arts and culture, education and the mass media.

What is worse, this politicization of religion and religionization of politics, had the full blessings of Hinduism, as interpreted by its most well respected exponents. From the very beginning, the Indian model of secularism was understood as a part of Hindu virtue of "tolerance" and "harmony". S. Radhakrishnan, India's president and noted philosopher, codified secularism in Hindu terms which have continued to influence its understanding to this date:

> " the religious impartiality of the Indian state is not to be confused with secularism or atheism. Secularism is here defined in accordance with the ancient religious tradition of India. ...it tries to build up the fellowship of believers...by bringing them into harmony with one another. This fellowship is based upon the principle of diversity [of religions] in unity [of attaining the highest spiritual truth].[23]

In other words, Hindus needed only to stay true to their faith in order to be secular. To make India more secular meant making it more Hindu. This is, indeed, the reasoning behind the infamous Hindutva ruling in 1996 by the Supreme Court which allowed candidates to invoke the Hindu nationalist idea of India as Hindu nation in election campaigns. In the opinion of Supreme Court Justice J.S.Verma, the promise to make India into a Hindu rashtra cannot be counted as an appeal to religion for votes because Hinduism is not a religion but a way of life of all Indians. What is more, according to Justice Verma, Hinduization of Indian culture poses no threat to the constitutional promise of secularism because "secularism in the Constitution is merely a reaffirmation and continuation of the Indian (i.e. Hindu) way of life." Secularism, in this reading, only requires a perpetuation of Hinduism.[24]

Can Hinduism really deliver a secular society, even when secular is understood in terms of the Indian interpretation of "equal treatment" and "tolerance" of different religions? The notion that plurality of gods makes Hindus uniquely tolerant and open-minded is more of a romance than serious history. What passes as tolerance in India has always been a variety of hierarchical inclusivism which simply treats the alien and the different as an inferior version of the metaphysical truths of the Vedas. Yes, we haven't had witch-hunts, but then we haven't treated other people with different ideas as serious partners in a dialogue either. The predominant Hindu creed has been, in the apt words of Achin Vanaik (1997: 149), "you have your truths and I have mine, and mine is the deepest truth!" (This creed has over time developed an additional clause: " you have your truth and I have mine, and mine is the deepest truth which is scientific and rational, and yours is not!). This is not respect and tolerance, but encompassment and stifling of the other. Neither does this "respect" for difference make Hinduism more rational or scientific, as is often claimed by its votaries, because the knowledge of the other is treated as valid within its own limited sphere which cannot challenge the knowledge of the totality of matter and spirit, which only Vedic Hinduism has access to.

Leaving the details of the Indian case aside for a moment, I want to draw out one very fundamental commonality between the American and Indian models. In both cases, a revolution was sanctified by tradition; a break from the past was justified as a continuation of the past. In America, the right to liberty which was in fact born out of the terrible wrongs of political repression of dissenters, was justified either by invocation of natural law or by invoking the God of the Bible. In India, the imperative of democracy that was in fact born of the terrible wrong of the caste society, and the imperative of tolerance that was in fact born of the terrible wrong of the partition, were both justified in terms of Hindu dharma. If, as Alan Dershowitz (2004) has argued recently, becoming secular means realizing that human "rights derive from wrongs" (that is, from our past experiences of injustice), and not from any power that is external to human experience, the American and Indian models of secularism are not grounded in a secular culture. Indeed, both are deeply ironic, since they justify the attempt to separate God from politics, or as in India, to reform the sacred laws of caste, by invoking the same God and dharma they are trying to move away from! What is missing in both cases is the development of a secular worldview that can anchor the secular laws of the land.

Here India is at a much greater disadvantage. As we saw above, in America, the secularist spirit of Jefferson and Paine did find a home after all – in the mainline Protestant churches. Liberal churches took the naturalist and scientific thinking of the 19th and 20th centuries seriously and began to teach a de-mystified, non-super naturalistic Christian doctrine, which tried to preserve the ethics of Jesus but not his miracles. Nothing comparable happened in India. Following the trends set by neo-Hindu reformers such as Vivekananda, Sri Aurobindo and the erudite S. Radhakrishnan, modern science was largely put to work not to critique but to defend the supra-naturalistic and supra-rationalistic worldview of orthodox Hinduism which teaches an enchanted nature knowable through intuitive insight of yoga. Unlike the synthesis of science and religion through the 19th and 20th century America which made room for a godless, naturalistic worldview, the Vedic synthesis downplayed the naturalistic picture of the world either as a Western-Christian idea or as "lower" knowledge. What emerged from the neo-Hindu synthesis of science and Vedas was a supra-rationalistic and supra-naturalistic view in which spiritualistic interpretations of evolution, vitalistic theories of biology and mystical interpretations of quantum physics were used to claim scientific support for a New Age-ish, occult worldview in which the spirit has primacy over matter. Thus gurus and priests thought nothing of invoking science, while teaching the same old superstitions. This view of modern science being in agreement with the Vedas has become a part of the commonsense of educated middle classes including the followers of miracle-working gurus who sell their stunts as "scientific". The modernist impulse that sought to demystify nature and knowledge did find a home in the neo-Buddhist movement started by Dr. Ambedkar, but failed to take off in the absence of support from non-dalit intellectuals and the educated middle classes in general.

The rationalization and disenchantment from within the religious establishment that took place in America for most of the 19th and early 20th centuries, simply has no equivalent in India.

Popular Religiosity and Religionization of Politics

Our examination of the American and Indian experiences clearly establishes that secularization of the civil society is not a necessary precondition for the creation and functioning of secular states. Deeply religious people can decide to give themselves constitutions which cut formal ties between states and religions.

But while state secularism in religious societies is possible, it is not sustainable. Secular states without secular civil societies are fraught with great risks. Contrary to social critics who support secularism as a sound constitutional principle, but who are suspicious of secularization as elitist and somehow disrespectful of ordinary people,[25]I will argue in this section that secularization is a necessary condition for the long-term survival of secular states. Democratic procedures alone, without a concomitant critique and containment of religion, can deliver power to religious political movements, which often have fundamentalist and/or nationalistic agendas.

This point has been argued recently by Nikki Keddie, the well known historian of Islam. Keddie argues persuasively that the level and intensity of popular religiosity must be treated as relatively autonomous factors in explaining the rise of religious- political movements. Most social scientists tend to explain growth of conservative religious-political movements as perfectly rational defense reaction of ordinary people who find their traditional mores under attack by the forces of modernization, globalization and secularization. But Keddie argues that socio-economic changes themselves cannot explain why religious fundamentalist movements gain force in some societies, and not in others at roughly the same level of development and facing roughly the same challenges of modernization. For example, why is China relatively free from political religions while India is not? Why is Canada relatively free from aggressive Christian fundamental-ism of the kind that is consuming the United States? We can get a better understanding of why fundamentalisms appear where they do by including religiosity as a relatively autonomous cause of political action, and not merely as a symptom of some other primary contradiction. Keddie offers the following hypothesis:

> Significant religious political movements …tend to occur only where in recent decades (whatever the distant past) religions with supernatural

> and theistic contents are believed in, or strongly identified with, by a large proportion of the population...Either ... a high percentage of the population identifies with the basic tenets of its religious tradition regarding its god or gods, its scriptural texts and so forth...or/and there is a widespread quasi-nationalistic identification with one's religious community as against other communities (Keddie, 1998: 702, emphases in the original).

In other words, other things being roughly equal, societies with higher levels of religiosity and nationalism will tend to be more prone to religious-political mobilizations. This hypothesis helps us understand the developments in America and India where religiosity and nationalism have tended to reinforce each other.

Because religion and politics answer very similar questions – namely, how shall we live? What binds us together? – it should come as no surprise that religious and political views tend to cluster together. One of the generalizations that sociologists of religion can safely make is that, to quote Andrew Kohut et al (2000: 4), "in all faiths, people who show high levels of religious commitment – that is, people who engage in traditional practices and hold to traditional beliefs – tend to be more politically conservative." In other words, theological conservatism tends to go together with political conservatism.

Not surprisingly, theological views can, and do, influence political choices. People make political choices based upon their socio-economic interests in a manner that is in accord with their ultimate beliefs derived from their understanding of their sacred traditions. Indeed, ultimate beliefs can, and often do, trump socio-economic interests, and people can be made to vote for religious values and/or identities, even when it goes against their material interests. Faith itself, and not merely its opportunistic manipu-lations by politicians, is a political force.

The 2004 elections in America demonstrate the workings of faith in politics. George Bush owes his second term to the devout Christians who overcame their denominational differences and voted their faith.

Two observations about the religious landscape of America are important to understand the dynamic of faith in politics: One, that there has been an intensification of traditionalist, theologically conservative beliefs and practices among evangelical and Catholic Christians in the recent past. This intensification of faith has contributed to what has been called the "diminishing divide" between church and state, with a larger proportion of Americans than ever before showing a readiness to breach the wall of separation. Two, the growth of traditionalist religiosity was the single most crucial factor that returned George W. Bush to power in 2004. To cite the findings of the influential Pew Center's Trends, 2005:

> the political fault-lines in the American religious landscape do not run along denominational lines, but cut across them. That is, they are defined by religious outlook rather than denominational labels… Traditionalists, whether evangelicals, mainline or Catholic, are more likely to be Republicans, while those who are eager to adapt their faith to modern beliefs or who are secular are more likely to be democratic (p. 28, emphasis added).

In other words, the more traditionalist you are in your religiosity, the more likely you were to support the Christian-nationalist agenda of George Bush and his neo-conservative advisers. Not class, not ethnicity, nor denomina-tional affiliation, but the degree of religiosity was most reliable predictor of voting behavior.

Countless surveys and opinion polls over the years have established some fairly stable parameters of religious make up of American population. White evangelical Protestants (including those who define themselves as fundamentalist) make up roughly a quarter of the US population, followed by 21 percent who belong to more liberal, mainline Protestant churches. Another 27.3 percent Americans are Catholics, 7.6 percent Black Protestants, 2 percent Jews and about 4.5 percent make up all the rest of believers, including Muslims, Hindus, Buddhists etc. Only a miniscule 1 percent are openly atheistic or agnostic.

One major change over time is the growth of the more theologically conservative, salvation-oriented evangelical churches at the expense of theologically modernist, this-worldly, liberal churches. Thus, between 1971 and 1990, evangelical churches gained more than 6 million new members, while the mainline churches lost some 2.6 million.[26]

But numbers tell only a part of the story. What is even more remarkable is that within all religious groups, there has been an intensification of traditional theistic, supernatural beliefs in the last ten years or so. According to Andrew Kohut and his colleagues who put together the panorama of religion in America in their 2000 book, The Diminishing Divide, from 1987 to 1997, there was a substantial increase in the portion of the public who strongly agreed with a belief in existence of god (from 60 to 71 percent), the inevitability of divine judgment (52 to 64 percent), the possibility of miracles even today (from 47 to 61 percent), the importance of prayer (from 41 to 52 percent) and the clear line between good and evil (from 34 to 45 percent). This increase in religiosity in recent years was across the board, among all Christian denominations and even among those who had no definite affiliation. This data is not broken up according to class or ethnicity. But knowing that the poor in America are nearly twice as religious as the rich (Norris, 2004: 108-110), and given that churches have historically served to soften the harsh realities of America's brutal capitalism, it is quite likely that this intensification of religiosity coincides with the intensification of poverty and insecurity in America in recent decades.

Not only have religious beliefs grown in intensity through the 1990s, the faithful also seem to have lost their earlier inhibitions about keeping faith out of the public sphere. A much cited Gallup poll showed that in 1968 a majority of Americans (53 percent) believed that churches should keep out of political matters, while 40 percent felt churches should express their views on day-to-day social and political questions. When the same questions were asked in 1996, the balance of sentiments was found to be reversed: 54 percent believed that churches should express their views, while 43 percent disagreed (Kohut et al, 102). It appears that the Jeffersonian wall of separation lasted as long as the traditional white Protestants wanted to deny any state benefits to Catholic schools. As Catholics and Jews have found greater acceptance in larger society, they are no longer seen as the enemy. Rather, the new alignment is that of the religious intense in all the traditional faiths against secular culture.[27] In that fight, traditional believers are only too keen on allowing the churches to get involved in policy making at all levels, and in all branches of the government. The only saving grace is that a majority of Americans still hesitate in having churches openly endorse political candidates from pulpits, even though plenty of direct politicking from the pulpit did take place in the last elections.

The growth in the intensity of traditional beliefs obviously does not automatically mean a growth in the fundamentalist style of religiosity. Indeed, more in-depth interviews with believers of varying religiosity show that most Americans still prefer a "quiet faith", which shies away from religious extremism and values toleration and individual freedom in matters of conscience (Wolfe, 1998).

But the growing intensity of religiosity does suggest a greater sympathy for conservative social values, including a faith in America's Manifest Destiny. Opinion polls consistently show that traditional religiosity goes hand in hand with political and social conservatism. The Pew Foundation's Trends 2005 clearly shows that those who attend church more frequently are significantly more opposed to gay marriages and stem cells research, two of the hot-button social issues that George Bush pushed with great deftness in the 2004 presidential campaign. The Trends report also shows a far greater support for the Iraq war and the "war on terror" among the more devout, as compared to the less committed and liberal Christians.

The Trends report also confirms one more feature of religiosity in America, namely, nationalism. As observers from Alexis de Tocqueville onward have noted, Christianity in America is deeply intertwined with American national identity. Religiosity and patriotism tend to cluster together: those Americans who profess deeper commitment to their faith also tend to be more nationalistic because they see their God and their country as inseparable (see Huntington, 2004). It is, moreover, a part of the American creed to see their country in messianic terms with a sacred mission to save the world. It is for this reason Americans have by and large bought George Bush's equation of 9/11 terrorists as enemies of civilization itself. This self-image of their nation as a redeemer nation, as literally doing God's work of spreading the light of liberty around the world constitutes one of the deepest ironies of American history, in which the impulse for the good turns into a force for imperialism and militarism. George Bush plays upon this self-righteousness when he says without even a trace of irony: "I am amazed that people hate us, because I know how good we are."[28]

India is another country where widespread religiosity tends to merge seamlessly into nationalism and patriotism. Like the Christian Right that views America as a Christian nation, Hindu nationalists insist on equating India with its Hindu-ness.

There is, of course, a world of difference between Hindu and American nationalisms. American nationalism is based upon political ideals, and not upon ethnic or racial origins. The American creed of individual liberty, constitutionalism, rule of law, political (but not economic) egalitarianism is assimilative, and at least in principle, open to all. What has made this creed so attractive around the world is its forward-looking and optimistic spirit. The American creed is not a product of past defeats and historic grudges, but promises a better life to all who come to its shores. This promise is becoming increasingly elusive, but its allure still holds.

Hindu nationalists dearly want to create an alternative Hindu-Indian creed which is as universally attractive, and even assimilative, as the American creed. This is what lies behind their tireless proselytizing, in countless ashrams and yoga-retreats in the West and increasingly in India, on behalf of lofty ideals of spiritual oneness, mind-body wholeness, Vedic sciences and ecology. This is the sanitized, romanticized and scienticized version of neo-Vedantic Hinduism they want to sell as an alternative to the supposedly failed materialism of the West. But, if you scratch the surface of this "liberal" façade, you come face to face with a deeply chauvinistic blood-and-soil nationalism which deifies the landmass of India either as the homeland of the "Aryans", or as the land where the "Aryan" culture found its fullest expression.[29] This notion of India as a sacred land where perennial wisdom was revealed often finds expression in literally turning the landmass of India into a Goddess (Bharat Mata). Only Hindus, for whom India is a sacred land as well as a native land, are considered the true sons and daugh-ters of Bharat mata, relegating Indian Muslims and Christians to the status of resident aliens. Underneath the image of tolerance and spiritual wisdom that Hindu apologists want to project, there is a simmering resentment (combined with envy) against all expressions of "Semitic monotheism".

As Koenraad Elst, a great admirer of Hindu nationalism describes it, unlike the Jews who had to first migrate to their motherland to found the Jewish state, the Hindus "merely had to remove the non-Hindu regimes from their territory. The Hindus are already in Delhi and merely have to change it to Indraprastha [the name of the ancient capital of Pandavas, the semi-divine heroes of Mahabharata]." The "non-Hindu regimes" that are targeted for removal from "Hindu territory" include the "Nehruvian and Islamic regimes from Pakistan" (p. 472). This is a succinct description of the anti-secularist and anti-Islamic sentiments that Hindu nationalists try to incite whenever they can.

The two sides of the Hindu nationalist project – the projection of Hindu virtues and the blood-and-soil nationalism – are not unrelated: they are two sides of the same coin. What unites them is popular Hindu religiosity. To use Nikki Keddie's thesis stated above, it is safe to say that the supernatural and scriptural beliefs that are prevalent among a vast majority of Indian people make it possible for the Hindutva ideology to appear plausible, noble and worthy of defense to a vast majority of Hindus. This does not mean that the ordinary believers are full of nationalistic passions, or that they can only be aroused to political action on religious grounds. All it means is that traditional religiosity of the voters remains a potential resource for political parties to mobilize for electoral gains.

Unlike the United States, good quantitative data on popular religiosity are hard to come by in India. There are hardly any comprehensive surveys of the religious convictions of the voters, and how these beliefs correlate with their political preferences. Media, travelogues and the emerging genre of non-fiction writing do occasionally give fairly good snap-shots of the ambiguities of popular religiosity, and how it intersects with the murderous politics of the Hindu rightwing in India.[30]

However, the lack of comprehensive data has not prevented prominent Indian intellectuals from passing judgments on the role of religiosity in politics. Their verdict: Hindu religiosity has nothing to do with Hindu nationalism. Hinduism and Hindu nationalism (or Hindutva) are seen as two entirely different kinds of belief systems. Real Hinduism is a faith and a way of life which has nothing to do with Hindutva, which is a modernist ideology, a political slogan. Or in another formulation, real Hinduism teaches universalism and tolerance, while Hindutva is a caricature of these ideals. Hinduism good, Hindutva bad; use good Hinduism to fight bad Hindutva – this is the dominant stance of secular intellectuals in India.[31]

Ironically, while secular intellectuals bend over backwards to exempt Hinduism from their critique of Hindutva, the Hindu nationalist camp is ever more alive to the importance of cultivating Hindu sensibilities for staging a comeback. Swapan Dasgupta (2005), one of the most astute sympathizers of Hindu nationalist causes, has recently issued a call for cultivation of an "evangelical Hindutva" which will harness the "little traditions" of ordinary Hindus, side-stepping the Brahminical institutions and personalities like the Shankracharya. The aim of "evangelical Hindutva" will be to cultivate more popular TV-preachers and gurus, India's equivalents of Billy Graham and Pat Robertson. It is the little traditions of Hinduism, harnessed by "earthy evangelists" – including some of the most vehemently anti-Muslim and anti-Christian preachers – that will provide the real energy for Hindu nationalists.

On this issue, I am afraid that the Hindutva side has it right and the secularists have it wrong. For all their differences, the psychological and behavioral manifestations of Hinduism and Hindutva are nearly identical. Yes, of course, Hindutva is not a religious movement, for it is not in the business of salvation of souls, or in the business of spreading god-awareness. It is in the business of acquiring power in order to bring its version of militant Hinduism as a blue-print for state policies. But that does not mean that the beliefs, values and symbols of Hinduism bear no relationship with the politics of Hindu nationalism. On the contrary, to an average Hindu the religious iconography, allegories and millenarianism (Ram Rajya) that Hindu nationalists use in their political mobilizations appear indistinguish-able from the real thing. The religiosity of ordinary Hindus predisposes them favorably to the symbolism and the message of Hindutva.

Examples are too numerous to count. When the Shiv Sena hosts Ganesh pujas in Muslim areas in Mumbai, don't believers come out to actually worship Ganesh? When the BJP took out the infamous yatra to Ayodhya, did not Ram's "chariot" develop a ceremonial life of its own? When India's map takes the form of a Goddess, an incarnation of Durga, does it not become an object of worship? When state legislatures host readings of Ramayana, do they not try to take on the aura of Ram Rajya?

Indeed, the link between religiosity and Hindu nationalism is not limited to idol-worship, the form of popular religiosity more common among ordinary people. The more elite, "intellectual" Hindus, who prefer gurus with a more eclectic mix of old and new Hindu doctrines, were no less supportive of Hindutva's cultural agenda, or immune from its chauvinism. Indeed, well-known modern gurus, including such charismatic figures as Sat Sai Baba, Amritanandmayi (Amma), Sri Sri Ravi Shankar, all lent their full support to Hindu nationalists when they were in power.

To think that religious faith is politically innocent is to take a very shallow view of faith. It is to deny that people do not respond to their immediate social-economic interests alone, but also to their ultimate concerns regarding what they consider sacred and morally meaningful.

To conclude this section, America and India offer valuable lessons regarding how rightwing nationalistic parties can come to power by mobilizing the power of faith. America and India also show the limits of secular constitutions which are not grounded in secular cultures. They show that democracy alone can't deliver a secular government that is indifferent to God. Indeed, in democracies where the levels of traditional, unreformed religiosity remain high, the logic of numbers will favor those parties that choose to foreground religious or "values" issues. As long as faith in traditional institutionalised religions remains high, religiosity will remain a potential ally of social conservatives and nationalist political parties.

Secular Culture for Secular Societies

At the end of the twentieth century, both religion and nationalism have outlived their obituaries. Both are alive, well and growing. God and country, never entirely separate to begin with, are coming together again in a combustible mix.

What is to be done? It is easy for secularists to despair, as in America these days, or to celebrate too soon, as in India where the Hindu right lost the last election. There is also the temptation to mobilize a "religious left" that can invoke sacred books to organize for social justice, peace and environmentalism. The idea is to use "good' religion to wean people away from "bad" religion, invoke the "real" faith to challenge those who would turn it into an "ideology" for war and hatred.

There is no doubt at all that the secular left does need to get religion right, but that does not mean that it must get religion. It is time for the secular left to take religion seriously, not as false consciousness, not as a left-over superstition from the past, but as a necessary dimension of human life which answers a nearly universal need for finding transcendent purpose in life and death. This need for meaning that can dignify the existential struggles of everyday life, and overcome the fear of death, is integral to human existence. The secularists must learn to respect this need for sacred meaning, and not rush to condemn every expression of religiosity as a sign of backwardness or superstition. Moreover, history furnishes many examples when transcendent meanings have motivated oppressed peoples to challenge the positive laws of their societies. Who can deny the influence of the Biblical narratives of Exodus and the innocent suffering of Christ on the Blacks' struggle for freedom from slavery in America? (However, the church was on both sides of the issue: the slaveholders also saw themselves as good upright Christians). Although the mainstream Sanskritic traditions of Hinduism do not have much to offer to those at the bottom of the heap, lower castes and women have found emotional sources for dignity and equality in the more "evangelical" bhakti traditions of Hinduism. Undoubtedly, a secularist left must develop a more well-rounded, less reductionist appreciation of religion in society that makes room for these manifestations of faith.

But while it is important to give faith its due, faith, too, must give reason its due. A secular society must respect religion, but only within the limits of reason. Because religious faith touches upon ultimate concerns of ethics and justice, it cannot be kept sequestered in the private sphere: as we have seen, the purely legalistic wall of separation between private faith and public reason is not sustainable. The reach of reason must extend to all empirical claims that derive from faith in the super-natural/spiritual entities and the sacred teachings derived from them, everywhere, whether in the public or in the private sphere. A wall of separation between reason and faith must go up in the minds of citizens first in order for the wall of separation to work in society.

In practical terms, this means a revival of the forgotten rationalist-skeptical elements of the secularist project represented by Jefferson and Paine in America and by Nehru, Ambedkar and Roy in India. Their secularist project meant not just a matter of laws and rules, but a matter of intellectual conviction. It was born of an inquiring attitude toward religion, aware of the great harm dogmatism in the name of God or dharma has caused through history, either through wars of conquest and colonialism or through the passive-aggressive violence of caste institutions.

Secularism as a worldview does not mean rejecting all sense of the sacred that transcends the profane world of here-and-now. But it does mean divesting the sacred of the right to make existence claims about entities which supposedly act in nature – soul, spiritual forces, reincarnation, miracles, to name a few. Or to put it more precisely, secularism means reserving the right to demand the same level of evidentiary support for those religious propositions which claim to represent some actual entities or processes in the actual world we reserve for other empirical beliefs. As long as the God of religions is supposed to be present in the world of space and time accessible to ordinary human senses, He/She/It has to be able to stand up to the same level of scrutiny as any other claim about empirical phenomena.

The entire tradition of inquiry that evolved out of the scientific revolution and the Enlightenment is crucial for the creation and deepening of a secular culture which does not accept authority on faith alone. The role of science in the development of a secular culture is not to create a new scientistic morality, but to challenge the aura of factuality, or naturalness, that all religions tend to clothe their symbols in. The religious attitude is one that holds the natural order as a moral order, either as expressing the God's laws (as in Abrahamic faiths) or as nature itself as being alive and purposeful (as in Hinduism). Either way, a religious culture looks for the basis of its moral order in something external to "mere" human experience. The importance of the modern empiricist modes of thinking that emerged out of the scientific revolution is that they challenge this essentially religious attitude which seeks to align affairs of this world with divine purposes revealed in nature's laws. The world of nature, as understood by the best scientific evidence we have, is devoid of any plans or purposes. This disgodding of nature and the realization that there are no divine commandments in nature, morality and politics is the fundamental pre-requisite for the emergence of a secular culture. Only such a culture can truly sustain a secular state.

The defense of secularism in our times must start with a defense of scientific reason itself. In recent times, modern science has come in for harsh and unwarranted criticism from the postmodern left for serving the ends of colonial and patriarchal powers that oppress the marginalized social groups. Modern science, according to its "radical" critics, is a social construct that makes the dominant interpretations of nature appear as if they were facts of nature. This radical skepticism toward the content of modern science has resulted in calls for "alternative sciences" which will produce a benign and socially progressive picture of nature from the standpoint of the non-dominant social groups. This enterprise of social construction of alternative accounts of nature has been a terrible diversion from the task of confronting the growing forces of reactionary religiosity. What is worse, this postmodernist deconstruction of science is very hospitable to the defenders of intelligent design in America who have been using very similar arguments to condemn naturalism of Darwinian evolution as a social construct of secular elites (Pennock, 2000).

A defense of the objectivity and universality of modern science is the first pre-requisite of the defense of secular culture everywhere. Scientists and freethinkers have no choice but to get more deeply engaged with intelligent design creationism and other Biblical and New Age superstitions that are gaining ground in America.

However, the need for a critical engagement with religious metaphysic is much more urgent in India. For reasons having to do with the history of colonialism and the nature of Hindu metaphysics, India has largely used modern science for purely instrumental purposes of research and industrial development on the one hand, and for largely apologetic purposes of defending Hinduism as scientific, on the other. Scientific temper has not had a rationalizing impact on the cultural-religious understandings of nature and knowledge.

While the rationalist and naturalist spirit of the Enlightenment found a hospitable environment in the mainline churches in America, it utterly failed to find a home in the Hindu establishment in India. On the surface, the neo-Hindu reformers of the 19th century "renaissance" were enthusiastic supporters of modern science – especially a vitalistic interpretation of evolu-tionary theories and contemporary, pre-quantum mechanics physics. But from the very beginning, Hindu thinkers, including world-renowned thinkers like Swami Vivekananda, Sri Aurobindo and S. Radhakrishnan, deployed science for the purpose of apologetics. Modern science was interpreted as affirming – belatedly – what was already known to the Vedic sages. The mechanical philosophy that had emerged from the scientific revolution was understood as only challenging the Christian God which stood apart from nature, but not the Hindu Brahman which was a part of nature. Christian God was seen as dying under the impact of science, and Hinduism was presented as the religion of the future which could unite reason with spirituality. Modern science was turned into a handmaiden of Hindu metaphysics. This tendency to scientize the sacred teachings of Hinduism has only grown in volume and in sophistication as it has joined forces with the holistic science, New Age, eco-feminist and pagan ideas in the West.[32]

Even more troubling is the complete absence of the Kantian separation of empirical knowledge of the phenomenal world from the supra-sensible realm which is in principle inaccessible to the human mind. Modern Hindu gurus have perpetuated the idea that human mind can access the world of "pure consciousness" or Absolute reality through mystical experiences. This has led to all kinds of absurdities flourishing in the mainstream of Indian culture all under the cover of "science". As I have tried to argue, these beliefs are not harmless: they are central to the strong current of chauvinism and Hindu nationalism that has widespread support in all sections of the Indian society.

To sum up: The future of secular societies depends upon the cultivation of secular culture. The real struggle against religious fundamentalism must start with a defense of science and reason.

Notes

1 This explanation about Robertson's resignation was offered by Gary Bauer and Ralph Reed, both well known leaders of the Christian Right. See Dana Milbank, "Religious Right Finds its Center in Oval Office", Washington Post, Dec. 24, 2001. The quote is

from Michael Farris, the Chairman of Home School Legal Defense Association, a Christian advocacy group. See Karen Tumulty and Matthew Copper, "What does Bush Owe the Religious Right?" Time, Feb 7, 2005.

2 Although the born-again population constitutes 38 % of the American population, it represented 53 percent of the vote cast in 2004 elections, supporting George Bush by a 62% to 38% margin. In contrast, non-born again voters supported John Kerry by an almost identical 59 percent to 39 % division. See the election update titled "Born Again Christians were a Significant Factor in President Bush's re-election" by the polling firm, Barna Organization at http://www.brana.org. The Catholic vote was even more crucial. Even though John Kerry is a Catholic, more Catholics voted for his opponent, George Bush: by a 52%-47% margin.See "It Wasn't Just (Or Even Mostly) the 'Religious Right'", Steven Waldman and John Green, http://www.Beliefnet.com. accessed April 20, 2005.

3 For an eye-opening account of the influence of Christian groups on the Bush administration, see Esther Kaplan, With God on their Side: How Christian Fundamen-talists Trampled Science, Policy and Democracy in George Bush's White House. New York: The New Press, 2004.

4 See "Did God Intervene?: Evangelicals are crediting God with securing the re-election of George W. Bush", Deborah Caldwell, Beliefnet.com. Accessed on Jan. 29, 2005.

5 For an annotated transcript of Bush's inaugural speech, see "Decoding Bush's God-Talk" on Beliefnet.com.

6 See report in the newsmagazine Outlook, Nov. 26, 2004.

7 For a chilling first hand account of how faith based initiatives actually work to favor the Christian Right, see Esther Kaplan (2004).

8 These figures are reported here from Lieven (2004) and Wolfe (1998).

9 For an extremely revealing portrait of the soul of a mega-church, see the recent article by Jonathan Mahler in The New York Times Magazine.

10 Barbara Harriss-White (2003) provides a detailed account of the role of religion in economic relations.

11 For recent case studies of newer forms of religiosity in India see John Harriss (2003) and Maya Warrier (2003).

12 I have in mind the classic writings of Donald Eugene Smith who used America as literally the gold standard for defining a secular state.

13 A recent statement of this conceptual separation between secularism and secularization appears in Jacobsohn (2003: 27-28). See also Rajeev Bhargava (1998: 489).

14 Here I must mention the writings of my friend Achin Vanaik (1997) who has written

forcefully on the priority of cultural secularization over formal secularism.

15 George Marsden (1990) is a good resource for understanding the inner tensions of the early Protestantism in America, as is the important book by Kramnick and Moore (1997). Stephen Carter (2000) offers a spirited defense of a "single-sided wall" that was meant to keep the state out of the church, but not the church out of the state.

16 For a critical appreciation of the influence of naturalism on American religion, see William Shea's important book The Naturalists and the Supernatural. In my previous work (2004), I have tried to show how this secular tradition influenced the worldview of India's own pre-eminent secularist, B.R. Ambedkar.

17 Scopes Trial

18 According to the well-known political theorist Cass Sunstein, constitutional democracies are strongly committed to "the anti-caste principle", which "forbids social and legal practices from translating highly visible and morally irrelevant differences into a systematic source of social disadvantage..." quoted here from Jacobsohn, p. 91.

19 Donald E. Smith's (1998) reflections on the legal provisions of secularism in the Indian Constitution still remain the best introduction to the subject.

20 For a solid secularist critique of the Indian brand of secularism as tolerance the best resource is Achin Vanaik (1997). See also Chatterji (1995) and Kesavan (2001). For anti-secularist critiques of secularism, see the writings of Ashis Nandy and T.N. Madan, both in Bhargava (1998).

21 See James Chiriyankandath (2000) for the debates in the Indian Constituent Assembly. The label "ameliorative secularism" is from Jacobsohn (2003).

22 See Stephen Carter (2000).

23 Quoted here from Chatterji (1995: 103).

24 Justice Verma made these observations in an interview with Gary Jacobsohn. See Jacobsohn (2003: 206-209).

25 Bhargava (1998) for example, and Carter (2000).

26 These figures are quoted from Lieven (2004: 140).

27 For an insightful analysis, see Jeffery Rosen's recent essay in New York Times Magazine.

28 It was Rienhold Niebuhr who warned Americans of the "ironic tendency of virtues to become vices when too complacently relied upon; and on the power to become vexatious if the wisdom that directs is trusted too complacently." Quoted here from Lieven (2004: 52). Lieven provides an excellent analysis of religious nationalism in America.

29 Vasant Kaiwar (2005) has shown that the older generation of Hindu nationalists as-

sumed that the "Aryans" came from elsewhere but found the fulfillment of their vision in India, while the contemporary Hindu nationalists are inclined to believe that India was the original homeland of the "Aryans". In either case, the notion of India as the cradle of "Aryan" culture has become a part of the cultural commonsense of a large number of educated Indians.

30 The recent writings of Suketu Mehta (2005) and Mukul Dube (2004) are good examples.

31 For a small but representative sample see Pratap Bhanu Mehta (1999), Amulya Ganguli (1999), Ashis Nandy (1998).

32 Indian critics of Hindu nationalism have not engaged in a sustained critique of "Vedic science". Except for their outspoken criticism of Vedic astrology, there have not been too many interventions in the matter of science. My book (Nanda, 2004) contains references to relevant literature on neo-Hindu apologetics.

References

Bruce, Steve, 2002. God is Dead: Secularization in the World. Oxford U.K.: Blackwell Publishers.

Bruce Steve, 1996. Religion in the Modern World: From Cathedrals to Cults. Oxford: Oxford University Press.

Bhargava, Rajeev. 1998. What is Secularism For? In Secularism and its Critics, edited by Rajeev Bhargava, 486-543. New Delhi: Oxford University Press.

Carter, Stephen. 2000. God's Name in Vain: The Wrongs and Rights of Religion in Politics. New York: Basic Books.

Chatterji, P.C. 1995. Secular Values for Secular India. New Delhi: Manohar.

Chiriyankandath, James. 2000. Creating a Secular State in a Religious Country: The Debate in the Indian Constituent Assembly. Commonwealth and Comparative Politics, 38 (2): 1-24.

Dasgupta, Swapan. 2005. Evangelical Hindutva. Seminar, 545, Annual Number, pp. 43-46.

Dershowitz, Alan. 2004. Rights from Wrongs: A Secular Theory of the Origins of Rights. New York: Basic Books.

Dube, Mukul. 2004. The Path of the Parivar. New Delhi: Three Essays Collective.

Elst, Koenraad. 2001. Decolonizing the Hindu Mind. New Delhi: Rupa.

Ganguly, Amulya. 1999. Hinduism and Hindutva, The Hindustan Times , Feb. 8.

Goel, Sita Ram. 2000. Defense of Hindu Society. New Delhi: Voice of India.

Harriss, John. 2003. When a Great Tradition Globalizes: Reflections on two studies of the 'Industrial Leaders' of Madras. Modern Asian Studies. 37(2): 327-362.

Harriss-White. 2003. India Working. Cambridge: Cambridge University Press.

Heimsath, Charles. 1964. Indian Nationalism and Hindu Social Reform. Princeton, NJ: Princeton University Press.

Hofstadter, Richard. 1962. Anti-intellectualism in American Life. New York: Vintage.

Huntington, Samuel. 2004. Dead Souls: The De-nationalization of the American Elite. The National Interest, March 22.

Hutchinson, William.1976. The Modernist Impulse in American Protestantism. Oxford: Oxford University Press.

Jacobsohn, Gary Jeffery, 2003. The Wheel of Law: India's Secularism in Comparative Constitutional Context. Princeton: Princeton University Press.

Jacoby, Susan. 2004. Freethinkers: A History of American Secularism. New York: Metropolitan Books.

Kaiwar, Vasant. 2005. The Aryan Model of History and the Oriental Renaissance: The Politics of Identity in an Age of Revolutions, Colonialism and Nationalism. In Antimonies of Modernity, edited by Vasant Kaiwar and Sucheta Mazumdar, Duke University Press, pp. 13-61.

Kaplan, Esther. 2004. With God on Their Side: How Christian Fundamentalists Trampled Science, Policy and Democracy in George Bush's White House. New York: Free Press.

Keddie, Nikki. 1998. The New Religious Politics: Where, When, and Why do "Fundamentalisms" Appear? Comparative Study of Society and History, 40(4): 696-723.

Kesavan, Mukul. 2001. Secular Common Sense. New Delhi: Penguin.

Kohut, Andrew, John Green et al, 2000. The Diminishing Divide: Religion's Changing Role in American Politics. Washington D.C: Brookings Institution Press.

Kramnick, Issac and R. Laurance Moore. 1997. The Godless Constitution: A Case Against Religious Correctness. New York: W.W.Norton.

Lieven, Anatol. 2004. America Right or Wrong: An Anatomy of American Nationalism. New York: Oxford University Press.

Madan, T.N. 1998. Secularism in its Place. In Secularism and its Critics, edited by Rajeev Bhargava, op. cit., pp.297-320.

Mahler, Jonathan. 2005. The Soul of the New Exurb. The New York Times Magazine, March 27.

Marsden, George. 1991. Understanding Fundamentalism and Evangelicalism. Grand Rapids, MI: William B. Eerdmans and Co.

Marsden, George. 1990. Religion and American Culture. Fort Worth: Hartcout Brace College Publishers.

Mehta, Pratap Bhanu. 1999. Hollow Hinduism: The VHP's Self-Defeating Vision. Times of India, Feb. 18.

Mehta, Suketu. 2004. Maximum City: Bombay Lost and Found. New York: Alfred A. Knopf.

Nanda, Meera. 2004. Prophets Facing Backward: Postmodernism, Science and Hindu Nationalism. New Delhi: Permanent Black.

Nandy, Ashis. 1998. The Politics of Secularism and the Recovery of Religious Tolerance. In Secularism and its Critics, edited by Rajeev Bhargava, op. cit., 321-344.

Norris, Pippa and Ronald Inglehart. 2004. Sacred and Secular: Religion and Politics Worldwide. Cambridge, UK: Cambridge University Press.

Pennock, Robert. 2000. Tower of Babel: The Evidence Against the New Creationism. MIT Press.

Pew Center for Religion and Public Life. 2005. Religion and Public Life: A Faith Based Partisan Divide, Trends 2005. Available at http://www. pewforum.org.

Rajaram, N.S. 1995. Secularism: The New Mask of Fundamentalism. New Delhi: Voice of India.

Rosen, Jeffery. 2000. 'Is Nothing Secular?' New York Times Magazine, January 30.

Roy, M. N. 1948[1968]. 'The Secular State'. In V.K. Sinha (ed.) Secularism in India. Bombay: Lalvani Publishing House.

Smith, Donald E. 1998[1963]. India as a Secular State. In Secularism and its Critics, ed. Rajeev Bhargava, op. cit., 177-233.

Shea, William. 1984.The Naturalists and the Supernatural. Mercer University Press.

Vanaik, Achin. 1997. Communalism Contested: Religion, Modernity and Seculari-zation. New Delhi: Vistaar Publication.

Warrier, Maya. 2003. 'Process of Secularization in Contemporary India: Guru Faith in the Mata Amritanandmayi Mission'. Modern Asian Studies, 37(1): 213-253.

Wolfe, Alan.1998. One Nation, After All. New York: Penguin Press.

HINDU ECOLOGY IN THE AGE OF HINDUTVA
Dangers of Religious Environmentalism in India[1]

Let me introduce the subject matter of this essay with a news story that appeared in The Frontline last year (June 2004). The story was about a prolonged drought in the Osmanabad district in the Western state of Maharashtra. In response to the dire shortage of water, the district officials invited 40 local non-profit organizations, including scientists and environmentalists from the famous Tata Institute of Social Sciences to organize a campaign to promote water conservation. Together they came up with the idea of pani yatra, or water pilgrimage: the organizers took a pot, filled it up with water from a 700-years old well, dressed up this pot with Hindu religious items (red cloth, garlands and coconuts) and took it around as they performed street plays regarding the importance of water conservation. According to the story, "people came out in large numbers to offer prayers to the water pot" as they took in the rest of the political theater. The accompanying photograph showed a throng of women offering prayers to the "sacred" water pot.

Now, this little episode was a perfectly innocent and well-meaning affair. It seems a bit unfair that I should single it out as an entry point for a critique of religious environmentalism. The organizers had best of intentions: they were mobilizing popular religiosity in order to promote water conservation. And what is wrong with that, you may well ask?

Here is what bothers me. Conservation of water, especially in the time of drought, has nothing particularly Hindu or particularly sacred about it: it is simply a rational thing to do, regardless of whether or not you believe in God, and regardless of whether you are a Hindu, a Muslim, a Christian or an alien from outer space who needs to drink water to live. But with pani yatra, water conservation was turned into an act of Hindu worship. The ecological became religious. Water, a scarce natural resource, became a sacred embodiment of gods. Environmental concerns were taken out of the secular realm, and turned over to the religious realm; the public space itself was turned into a makeshift temple. All this happened with the willing cooperation of environmental activists many of whom, in all likelihood, pride themselves in being secular.

But one could still ask, so what? What is wrong with making the ecological religious? Why should religion not have a role in environmental protection? Why shouldn't new social movements tap the popular religiosity of ordinary people for environmental protection?

The aim of this essay is to lay out a case, as clearly as I can, why new social movements should refrain from invoking religion, even for the worthy cause of protecting the environment.

2.

Following Ram Guha's well-known typology, there are three main tendencies in Indian environmentalism: the greens, the eco-developers and the managers. The green politics in India, unlike its counterpart in the West, is not a middle-class, largely conservation-oriented phenomenon. Instead, protection of the environment is fundamental to ensuring economic livelihood and social justice for the vast majority of people who still make a living in subsistence agriculture.

Now, campaigns resembling pani yatra are standard fare in ecological activism in India. In order to mobilize the masses, Indian greens have not shied away from invoking Hindu imagery and myths. The inherent sacredness of rivers, trees, animals and other natural entities is widely and routinely invoked in the Indian ecological movements, especially by such world-renowned environmentalists as Vandana Shiva and Sundar Lal Bahuguna of the Chipko fame, Baba Amte and Medha Patkar of the Narmada Bachao Andolan, even occasionally by members of the CSE, India's best known environmental clearing house, to say nothing of the countless lesser known activists and intellectuals who agitate on behalf of the natural environment. The assumption behind this turn to gods is that women, peasants, native people – who constitute the bulk of laboring classes in the country – will be mobilized to take care of trees and rivers and animals because they see them as sacred abode of gods, as embodiment of shakti.

Just about every popular Hindu ritual or idea has been tapped for its potential for mobilization on behalf of the environment. Examples range from women tying rakhis to trees, mass recitations of Bhagavat purana at the site of Chipko, fasts, and religious vows on the river banks and temples, circumambulating rivers and doing arti to them, invocations of God Krishna as the lord of cows and pastures, invocations of shakti, devi, bhu mata (or Narmada mata, or Ganga mata), karma, reincarnation. Even castes, or jatis, have been reinterpreted as biological species living in harmony with their environment. Gods are not limited to environmentalism alone: we now have temples devoted to AIDS-amma, a new goddess who has been created purposely to enhance "AIDS awareness".[2] And invocation of gods is not limited to NGOs/activists: district magistrates, government bureaucrats have not shied away from bringing in priests to do arti when they inaugurate municipal taps, all with the justification of promoting an awareness of the sacredness of natural resources.[3] A god – or more "feminist" yet, a goddess – for every season and every cause under the sun seems to be the general idea.

This is not my own "rationalist fundamentalist" reading of the state of environmental activism in India. Christopher Key Chapple, who has edited a major anthology on Hinduism and ecology arrives at the same conclusion: "in India, from the outset, there has been an appeal to traditional religious sensibilities in support of environmental issues" (Chapple, 1998: 20). Likewise, the UCLA-based historian Vinay Lal (2000), finds Indian environmentalism to have deeply imbibed the "too deep for deep ecology" worldview of Mahatma Gandhi which had its roots in a romanticized version of Hinduism. According to Lal, Gandhian philosophy has been the conduit through which a deep green shade of Hinduism has found its way into environmentalist movements, not just in India but in the West as well. I will elaborate on the shared philosophical ground between Hinduism and deep ecology later in the essay.

One can only speculate the reason why religiosity became a popular tool for environmentalism, though it is my impression that the reign of Hindutva through the 1990s has – finally – succeeded in tempering the new social movements' enthusiasm for invoking the sacred for secular objectives. It is nearly impossible to fathom the genuineness and the depth of the religious sentiment of environmental activists themselves. But there is no denying that the stresses on the natural environment in India are real, and the scale of displacement and suffering caused by competition over resources is enormous. It is understandable that activists would want to tap into popular religiosity in order to encourage sustainable pattern of development. In all this hectic activism, the question that does not get asked is whether popular religiosity can really promote an ecological ethic in the contemporary times. I will return to this question later in the essay.

3.

In this essay, I want to raise some fundamental questions regarding the use of Hindu symbols, rituals and cosmology in environmental activism in India.

My first set of concerns has to do with the dangers of co-option of Hindu environmentalism by Hindu nationalism. The Hindu idiom used by environmental movements and their academic apologists is indistinguish-able from the Hindu nationalist celebrations of dharmic ecology. Under the BJP government, dharmic ecology had already become a back-door through which Hindu temples and cults were being financed by the tax-payers money.

But that is not worst of it. Hindu nationalists have been actively seeking out alliances with a host of neo-pagan movements that are trying to revive the pre-Christian Celtic and Nordic gods in Europe and North America. The Western neo-pagans for the most part are quite content with their own pre-Christian traditions of local gods and rituals, but some of them are naturally attracted to Hinduism as a living example of polytheistic faith where gods are not remote from nature. This shared belief in the intrinsic sacredness of nature, or nature as "the body of God", with or without the traditions of yoga and Vedanta thrown in, is what brings the neo-pagans and Hindu nationalists together.

There is, of course, no reason why neo-pagans should not want to revive what they think are their ancient traditions. Pagans have as much right to create and propagate their gods as any other religion. There is also no reason why they should not seek to build bridges with Hinduism which they find more compatible with their way of thinking. After all, today's European neo-pagans are only walking in the footsteps of theosophists and romantics of an earlier era who sought out India as an antidote to the Western "decadence" brought on by the Enlightenment and the industrial revolution.

What concerns me is the very real danger of the emergence of an axis of ethnic-cultural nationalism based upon a combination of a genuine nature religion mixed with leftwing ideas of ecological protection on the one hand, and rightwing nativist ideas of organic nationalism on the other. Moreover, I see in the emerging alliance a new axis of "traditionalism", which can only encourage the kind of reactionary modernity we have had a taste of under the BJP rule. As described by Mark Sedgwick in his recent book, Against the Modern World, traditionalism is a belief, first put forward by the French philosopher Rene Guenon in the 19th century, that the modern world is in a state of crisis because it has lost the eternal spiritual truths – the so-called perennial philosophy – which were known to ancient peoples in the Orient and to the pre-Judeo-Christian civilizations of Europe. Traditionalist followers of Guenon believe that only a recovery and reinstatement of the perennial tradition can save the modern world from its inevitable death. In this drama, the East, especially India, has a starring role for it is seen by the traditionalists as a repository of eternal spiritual truths, the ur-religion of all of humanity, or what our own gurus would simply call sanatan dharma. It would indeed be wonderful if the spiritual traditions of India (or the pre-Christian Europe) could genuinely help make the world a better place – I will be the first to sign on. But the track record of Hindu spiritual truths at home hardly inspires much confidence. And if the experience of the last time when theosophists and other Western seekers of eternal truths turned to India for an "Oriental Renaissance" is any guide, there is plenty to fear from the emerging neo-pagan-Hindu nexus.[4]

My second big worry is the dangers of closing off secular spaces. I start with a simple question: why is pani-yatra OK, if we think that Advani's Rath yatra in 1990 which led to the destruction of the mosque in Ayodhya was not? Why should we, as scholars, activists and concerned citizens keep quiet or even applaud when environmentalists inject religion into public debates over red-green issues, when we condemn the Hindutvawadis for injecting Ram into the existence of the mosque in Ayodhya? Just because we believe – correctly – that our red-green goals are morally superior to their saffron ones, does it make it acceptable for us to invoke religiosity in matters related to resource use and economic development? Does the perceived nobility of our ends justify the means? Shouldn't secularism begin at home? Shouldn't we demand a separation of faith and politics in new social movements, just as much as from the Sangh Parivar, or from the current Congress parivar? Should we allow environmentalism to become an agent of Hinduization of politics and culture? (These problems are not unique to India: environmentalists in America are beginning to face similar dilemmas as evangelical Christians are beginning to turn green on the basis of their Biblical belief in the human duty to protect God's creation.)

But my third worry goes beyond the issues raised by the rise of the Hindu right wing. Suppose there were no Hindu nationalism. Suppose there was no danger of neo-pagan-new right connection. I would contend that using unreformed Hindu tradition for promoting an ecological conscious-ness would still be problematic because of the in-egalitarian, illiberal, irrational elements of the tradition. It is important to remember that the same world outlook that has learned to parade in the shades of deep green also directly legitimizes innate, natural hierarchies between human beings as part of nature's sacred laws.

In the rest of the essay, I hope to touch upon these issues, perhaps not in the exact same sequence in which I have just stated them. I will start with a brief description of the non-theistic, pantheistic, pagan spiritualism that has become the dominant ideology of environmentalism both in the West and in India. Then, using the example of Chipko, I will show that the use of Hindu idiom by the environmental movements has become the Trojan horse for Hindutva. Next, I will move on to the issue of the emerging alliance between European neo-pagans and Hindu nationalists. Finally, I will try to make a case for a secular and rational basis for environmental action in India. I will argue that sacredness of nature has not led to greater care of nature in Indian society. Just because people venerate trees and rivers does not mean that they will take care of them.

4.

In her recent book, Reconsidering Nature Religion, Catherine Albanese cites the following data:

- o 32 percent of environmental activists in the US are secularists, that is, they think that nature is important but not sacred in itself.
- o About 25 or so are Christian theists, that is, they think that nature is sacred because it was created by God.
- o The largest percentage, about 40 percent are pantheistic eco-spiritualists, that is, they think that nature is sacred in itself because it is animated by the presence of cosmic life force.

Bron Taylor (2001) a well known scholar of nature religions in America who has participated in the Earth First! and other radical groups, refers to the last category on Albanese's list as "pagan environmentalism" to convey the vast range of earth-based spiritualities from deep ecology, eco-feminism, and New Age to witchcraft (wicca), Celtic Druidism, Nordic Asatru and other practices oriented around ancient pre-Christian, native American or Eastern gods and goddesses. In her classic, Drawing Down the Moon, Margot Adler describes a complete mutuality between neo-paganism as a religion and neo-paganism as a philosophy of environmental action: a majority of those who join the "craft" (wicca) are motivated either by feminism or by ecology, and a majority of those who come to pagan faiths for whatever reason, express a commitment to protecting nature because of its inherent sacredness.

Pagan environmentalists would easily make up the largest and the fastest growing wing of the green movements around the world if we include the burgeoning Indian environmentalism to it. As I have already indicated the idea that nature is sacred in itself is widespread in India. In recent years, prominent academics and philosophers have backed the ecological activism in India by giving philosophical justifications for Hinduism's unique ecological sensibilities.

All eco-spiritualities – in the West and in India – share three features which stem from the deep disillusionment with the Enlightenment project that insisted on secularizing nature and politics.

- One, they seek immanence, situated-ness, localism and social constructed-ness for everything, including their conception of gods and their conception of what constitutes science (or truth, more broadly). Transcendence and universalism are condemned in both sacred and secular realms as sources of leveling and homogenization which silences the "other". To the extent that postmodernism has been defined as a suspicion of universal meta-narratives, pagan environ-mentalism is postmodern.
- Two, they are non-dualists. Because they see all things as manifestations of the divine, they reject distinctions between the spiritual and material, sacred and secular, humans and gods, or humans and other species. This leads in the direction of a thorough-going re-enchantment of nature, along with a thoroughgoing rejection of humanism.
- Three, they are opposed to anthropocentrism or humanism. Nature is to be protected and treated with care, not because it is a "resource" for human beings but because each element of nature has its own right to exist. Human beings have no special claims on nature. This belief in the intrinsic worth of all life, regardless of its usefulness for human beings, is the central moral claim that holds the diverse groups of activists with widely different political visions together in the radical environmental and anti-globalization movements.

Exact numbers are not known, but many in the deep-ecology/pagan environmentalist camp are either practicing Hindus, or at least profess a great affinity for Eastern spiritualities, including Buddhism and New Age ideas. It is well known that Arne Neass, the father of deep ecology, was deeply influenced by Advaita Vedanta and the writings of Gandhi and Sri Aurobindo. Non-dualistic monism of Vedanta has encouraged a kind of rational mysticism in New Age circles in the West through the writings of Fritjof Capra and Ken Wilber, along with voices from India, including the ecological writings of Vandana Shiva and the "quantum mystical" ideas made popular by people like Mahesh Yogi, Deepak Chopra and Amit Goswami. (The New Age is only one element of the ensemble of movements that differs from, but also complements, neo-paganism. While both believe in a lack of separation between spirit and matter, the New Agers are given to treating the real world as an illusion, while neo-pagan gods are present here and now in the real world of matter. As Michael York (1996:164) puts it, "paganism constitutes the this-worldly grounding of the New Age.")

Interestingly, Hinduism can justifiably lay priority claims on both the neo- pagan this-worldliness and the New Age other-worldliness that are so celebrated in deep ecology thought. Hinduism is a religion of nature. Traditional Hindu texts teach that the natural world is not just dead matter, but rather the body of God: the same spirit variously called purusha, shakti, atman, Brahman that animates human beings, animates all natural objects, living or non-living, big or small, from the humble rocks and rivers to bacteria and trees. Thus all entities of nature are alive, animated and deeply connected to all others. At a more philosophical level, Vedantic Hinduism teaches that all distinctions between the sacred and profane, spirit and matter are illusionary, because all that exists is a manifestation of the Brahman, or the World Spirit.

Those who extol this great divination of nature and man do not want to talk about the dark side of this enchanted, non-dualistic worldview. Yes, all things are pervaded by the same cosmic force, but not to the same extent, not equally. Brahman, or its feminine form, Shakti, so beloved of feminists takes on different gunas, or qualities, of lightness, darkness and energy based upon the karma of the jiva in all previous lives. All species are inter-connected, but this interconnected-ness is sustained by a constant cycling of atman through reincarnation, which assigns your soul to a species whose position in the chain of beings varies – from a rock to a cockroach to a man – in proportion to your karma in all your previous lives. All of nature is the body of God, but the feet of the body of God constitute the shudras: just like feet come in contact with dirt, so must the shudras. The immanent, all-pervasive consciousness is a source of holistic knowledge obtained through "direct realization", but it is also provides a cover for countless charlatans and god-men that have kept human intellect in chains for millennia. True, consciousness and matter are not separable, but it also means that consciousness, and morality based upon one's level of consciousness, have cosmological consequences. It also means that ordinary observant Hindus are directed by their religious teachings to regulate their lives in a manner that will sustain the cosmic order. There is nothing more stultifying and mind-numbing than this injunction to live by the order of nature and/or obey the social taboos out of fear of cosmic consequences. The horrendous inequities and superstitions that follow from this worldview somehow fail to register on the neo-pagan/New-Age mindset of pagan environmentalists, for they tend to see inequities as natural "differences" in the chain of being which must be preserved against the onslaught of capitalist mass society.

This, then, is my fundamental philosophical problem with eco-spiritualism that animates Hinduism and neo-pagan philosophies alike: it is grounded in a worldview that divinizes nature, or treats the natural law as sacred. In this worldview, egalitarianism and universalism are treated as unnatural, and therefore misguided, to put it mildly.

Are my worries overblown? I agree that neo-Hindu philosophers have been at pains to find support for human equality within Vedantic monism (all are one in Brahman). But I am not convinced that the ideas so eloquently expressed by Guru Golwalkar, below, have lost their grip on Indian culture:

> It is in this sense, i.e., the same spirit being immanent in all, that all men are equal. Equality is applicable only on the plane of the Supreme Spirit. But on the physical plane, the same spirit manifests itself in wondrous variety of diversities and disparities.
>
> According to our philosophy, the very projection of the universe is due to a disturbance in the equilibrium of three attributes – sattva, rajas and tamas. If there is a 'gunasamya' – a perfect balance of the three attributes – then the Universe will dissolve back into the Unmanifested State. Thus disparity is an indivisible part of nature and we have to live with it. Our efforts should be only to keep it in limits and take away the sting out of it.
>
> So any arrangement that tries to remove the inherent disparities on the basis of superficial equality is bound to fail....The concept of democracy as being "by the people" and "of the people," meaning that all are equal shares [sic] in the political administration, is, to a very large extent, only a myth in practice (Golwalkar, 1966, chapter III, emphases added).

Those who see only love and lightness in nature mysticism must not close their eyes to its dark side. If protecting the environment means adopting a worldview which has a long history of supporting deeply inegalitarian and anti-humanistic ideas, I recommend that we think twice. The price is simply too high.

5.

Leaving the larger philosophical issues aside for the moment, let me turn to a concrete case of environmental activism in India that has become an icon of Hinduism's unique eco-spirituality. I am referring here to the case of the Chipko movement.

The history of Chipko has been told many times. Chipko began as a movement to protect trees from commercial timber contractors in the Tehri Garwhal district in early 1970s. It was the local women's act of hugging the trees to protect them that made Chipko an icon of Third World women's ecological activism around the world.

A major part of the reason why Chipko came to grip the imagination of environmentalists and feminists around the world was that it was presented as an example of the superior ecological wisdom of India's peasant women. The well known writings of Vandana Shiva and the Gandhian Sudarlal Bahuguna absorbed Chipko in a narrative of India' unique spiritual heritage which regards nature as divine and sentient. Shiva and her fellow eco-feminists added the feminist angle by turning Chipko into an exemplar of third world women's unbroken inter-connections with the web of life. Nearly all the themes of pagan environmentalism that we have examined above found a vivid expression in the image of women hugging the trees.

But the Gandhian-ecofeminist romance put forth by Shiva and her colleagues was not an isolated case of myth-making. An entire genre of what has been described as "new traditionalist discourse" (Guha et al., 1997) emerged in India that contrasted the ecological wisdom of local traditions (which almost always turned out to be Hindu) with the depravity of modern industrial resource-use policies, many of them inherited from colonial times. The pre-colonial traditions in agricultural production, forestry and water-use were invariably presented as socially harmonious, eco-friendly and practically exuding a conservation ethic. In their numerous and influential writings, Madhav Gadgil and Ramachandra Guha popularized the notion that the institution of caste was a rational social arrangement that led to conservation of natural resource. They also singled out sacred groves – that is, groves or gardens, often owned by temples, dedicated to the exclusive use of gods and goddesses – as traditional means of conserving forests and promoting bio-diversity. Here were two of the most exclusive and most inegalitarian social institutions which had served to maintain the stranglehold of orthodox, upper caste Hinduism throughout India's history, and both were made to look like rational adaptations for resource management. Indeed, one could not help but wonder why, if these institutions were so rational and so ecological, they should not be brought back. Given the scale of deforestation, why shouldn't we ask temples to take over public forests and turn them into sacred groves? And if caste institutions have been so ecologically rational, why fight against them? Why not officially reinstate them?

That this traditionalist account of ecological history is factually flawed (Subir Guha et al., 1997) and that the ownership of forests by gods did not really prevent economic exploitation by the village elites (Freeman, 1999) has now been well established. Studies by Emma Mawdsley (1998) and Haripriya Rangan (2000) who revisited the Chipko area after the environmental bandwagon had moved on, have shown that the aftermath of Chipko was actually quite problematic for the local people who ended up starting a "cut down the trees" campaign in what is now Uttarakhand.

Be that as it may, for most of the final quarter of the twentieth century, the romance of traditions held sway among intellectuals.

Lately, this new traditionalism of environmentalist activists and historians has taken an explicitly High-Hindu turn. The theme of ecological wisdom of traditions drew the attention of sanskritists, Indologists and other scholars of religion. Two major anthologies, one under the auspices of Harvard Divinity School, appeared in quick succession (see Nelson, 1998, Chapple and Tucker, 2000). The magazine Hinduism Today took up the cause, as did the magazine of the Hare Krishna, Back to Godhead. Suddenly we started seeing interpretations of High-Hindu texts, everything from the Rig Veda to the Upanishads, along with Manusmriti, Bhagavat Gita, Bhagavat Purana, Ramayana, Mahabharata and even Shankara's Vedanta – one of the most idealistic, world-denying philosophies – as supporting a unique eco-spirituality suitable for the challenges of the 21st century world. We started to read karma, reincarnation and caste as sources of ecological wisdom. There were critical voices here and there, but the general tone of this explosion of Hinduism and ecology literature was celebratory: dharmic ecology could heal the environment inflicted by modern technology and capitalism. Hinduism had found a new worldwide mission: to save Mother Earth.

No overt sympathy can be discerned, at least from the writings, between this Dharmic ecology literature and the politics of Sangh parivar. This literature can be usefully read as providing a philosophical-theological supplement to the new-traditionalist history and activism already in full swing. The same ecological history of caste or sacred groves that had been touted by the environmentalists seeking indigenous models for ecological actions was now given theological support by finding some Sanskrit shloka from the Vedas or from any of the many sacred books. The intervention of so many Indologists and religious studies scholars, not known for their political activism, shows the high visibility Indian ecological movements had achieved in the academia in the United States. Especially notable was the near mythic status Chipko was assigned in the Hindu ecology literature.

Thanks to the painstaking and careful research by scholars like Rangan (2000) and others, it is by now very clear that Chipko was not an assertion of traditional values or even traditional forest rights of non-modern villagers and women against commercial forestry. Chipko was not a rejection of commercial forestry but a struggle for a preferred access to markets, credit, jobs and subsidies for the local people in the industry.

In the Hindu ecology literature, however, none of these critiques mattered. Vandana Shiva's and Sundarlal Bahuguna's interpretations of Chipko as the civilizational and religious expression of women and hill people are taken as canonical. Chipko is presented in the Hindu ecology literature as the application of foundational ideas of Hindu philosophy to environmental action and an "affirmation of spiritual value of nature". The recitation of Bhagwat Katha at the site of the original Chipko resistance, probably arranged by Sundar Lal Bahuguna, and women tying rakhi to trees are taken as evidence of the influence of Hindu religiosity. All the many issues of livelihood, class, gender were forgotten and the struggles of poor people were turned into an expression of religiosity which, in turn, was turned into an affirmation of the ancient wisdom of our Hindu sages.

Meanwhile, on the ground, the then BJP government and its VHP allies were showing that the two can play the same game: what works for the greens, also looks good in saffron. Ecological protection became one more channel for bringing Hinduism into the public realm, using pretty much the same language, the same symbols and occasionally even the same personalities of the environmental campaigns of Chipko and against the Narmada dam. As the eye-opening reporting by Mukul Sharma (2001, 2002) has shown, the anti-Tehri dam campaign launched by VHP shared many of the metaphors and rituals popular among mainstream environmentalists.

Under the BJP rule, government began to actively fund temples, pilgrimage sites and religious cults for reforestation and maintenance of sacred groves. A few examples will suffice:

- G. B. Pant Institute of Himalayan Ecology has been working with the temple of Badrinath. Scientists produce the saplings, the priests bless them and distribute them as prasad.
- Indian government funded in part the work of ISKCON (Hare Krishna) in re-forestation of Vrindavan. Again, tree planting is made into a sacred ritual, as prasad.

o Department of Environment is supporting temples to maintain sacred groves.

o Ecological aspects of Sanatana dharma have been included in the school text books of at least one state, UP.

6.

So far, we have looked at how the apparently secular environmental movement in India, which attracted so many activists of progressive and feminist persuasion from all over the world, increasingly turned to indigenous traditions in search for solutions to India's ecological crisis. We have seen how gradually and imperceptibly, the new traditionalism of the environmentalists came to be absorbed into the discourse of Hindu or dharmic ecology. We then examined how dharmic ecology informed the communal activism of BJP/VHP which turns rivers and forests into religious heritage of Hindus alone.

But there is yet another layer of Hinduization, an even deeper shade of saffron, which connects the discourse of Hindu ecology and sacredness of nature with neo-pagan movements that we examined earlier. The Hindu-neo-pagan dialogue is still in its initial stages, and may not amount to anything more than one more Western fringe religion looking for inspiration from Hinduism and India. But this relationship has the potential for a lot of mischief in terms of encouraging a chauvinistic blood-and-soil nationalism which claims that each race or ethnic group is entitled to the land of its own Gods. Given the deep currents of anti-Islamic sentiments 9/11 has released in America, Europe, to say nothing of India, the prospects of paganism turning into a diatribe against Islam and the other universal "stateless" religion, namely, Christianity (especially in India) are not all that far-fetched.

This is what is happening: As we saw in the last essay, Western Europe has gone much further in rejecting traditional Christianity than the United States. There has been a sharp decline in church attendance in both Protestant and Catholic countries. At the same time, with the collapse of the Soviet Union, combined with the growing doubts about the secular worldview of the Enlightenment, Europe is becoming increasingly post-Christian and post-rational. The intellectual and spiritual vacuum is being filled increasingly with a revival of pre-Christian pagan traditions, mostly of Europe's own classical pasts, including such traditions as the Viking or Norse mythology from the Scandinavian countries, the Celtic tradition of Ireland and the British Isles. Similar trends are visible in Eastern Europe as well. The fall of the Communist party has not automatically meant the resurgence of traditional Eastern Orthodox churches. Instead, many in Russia and Lithuania are turning to pagan and other esoteric traditions which were suppressed by the Church. The United States, where Christianity has held its ground, is also seeing a variety of new pagan religions, derived from a combination of Norse gods, wicca, native American and Asian traditions. The numbers do not even make a blip on the census data in America which remains an overwhelmingly Christian country. But the important point is that the numbers are growing.

As I discussed above, under the panoply of different gods and rituals, neo-pagans are united in their belief in the multiplicity of gods who can be "directly experienced" here-and-now through nature and through ritual. Pagans believe that by bringing the local gods and spirits of the land back, by re-enchanting nature, they can feel more rooted in the land of their gods and ancestors, and more connected with all the creatures that inhabit the landscape. Pagan eco-spirituality, in other words, is able to combine genuine ecological concerns with a desire for identity, roots and nationalism that seems to be growing in the face of growing globalization.

What seems to be emerging, to paraphrase Bron Taylor (2002: 63), is a "global bricolage", a "melting pot" of pagan environmental-political radicalism in which "diverse new and alternative religious ideas, rites, values, and actions, newly invented or borrowed from diverse traditions, places and times, cross-fertilize with modern ecological understanding and a host of anti-establishment causes and ideologies." What is of concern to me, as to many other students of this stew of ideologies,[5] is the possibility of cross-fertilization of ideas between genuine spiritual seekers, the politically progressive anti-racist environmentalist, and the radical religious nationalists. Those belonging to the last category share the pagan philosophy of the other two groups, but give it a radically ethno-nationalistic turn: they believe that each ethnic group (defined these days by culture, not by biological race) has its own Gods, which make their home in specific nations and landscapes. The ethnic pagans believe that each group must stick to the gods which are organic to their homeland and to their ancestors. This philosophy ends up as celebrating, in the name of multiculturalism and localism, the right of White people to have their own homeland. Or as a controversial advertisement that found its way into the pages of Earth First! proclaimed, " Now White Boys can be tribal, too!"[6]

Even though some fringe elements of ethnic pagans in America might be attracted to tantric rituals or to the neo-Nazi writings of Savitiri Devi, they have – mercifully! – not shown any obvious interest in India or Hinduism. But on the other hand, there seems to be plenty of cross-fertilization going on between European neo-pagans and Hindutva intellectuals. India has always had its share of spiritual seekers from the West – from the Beatles onwards – finding their personal gurus who help them along with their enlightenment. But the contemporary Hindu-pagan alliance is more overtly political and more full of proselytizing zeal. It is being led by the intellectual architects of Hindutva including such leading lights as the late Ram Swarup and Sita Ram Goel. The journal Hinduism Today has joined in, opening its pages to pagan groups from Russia, Lithuania, Ireland, Britain and Belgium.

By itself, there is no reason to be suspicious of this still evolving relationship. Hindus have as much right to propagate their faith and to attract new adherents as any other religion. And, likewise, European neo-pagans have as much right to seek out like-minded believers as any other group bound by ideas. But all is not light and harmony. If you scratch the surface, you can see wider connections and worldview affinities with the philosophy of the European new right. These philosophies are not racist in the old sense of overt biological racism. They are dangerous nevertheless because they have learned to co-opt the left-liberal ideas of tolerance, multiculturalism, anti-capitalism, scientific temper and environmentalism into a worldview which is deeply irrational and illiberal. They have learnt to cover their national-religious chauvinism in the language of the "right to be different" against the arrogant universalism of the West.

Let me illustrate these concerns with an example. Christopher Gerard is a Belgian pagan who has written movingly about how learning about Hindu dharma helped him discover this identity which had been "repressed first by the imprint of centuries of Christianity [and] then with the stamp of materialism." Gerard edits the journal Antaios, a journal of "polytheistic studies", in which he has published interviews with Hindu intellectuals, the late Ram Swarup and Sita Ram Goel. He acknowledges the influence of these intellectuals, especially Ram Swarup's, on his own thinking. His great admiration and love for Hinduism is obvious, and obviously sincere.

Interestingly, but not surprisingly, the remarks he made at a Hindutva event in Delhi in 2000 can be found posted on the website of Alain de Benoist, the founding father of the neo-paganist New Right in France.[7] Antaios, the journal Gerard edits, was founded by Mircea Eliade and Ernest Junger, the former with substantial links with Romanian fascism, and the latter with Nazism. I don't intend to raise the fascist bogey by putting too much weight on these links. I understand that de Benoist's New Right is different from old-time fascism of the centralized totalitarian state running concentration camps. I understand that the sins of the fathers with fascist sympathies (Eliade and Junger) cannot be visited upon their intellectual heirs like Christopher Gerard. What interests me is the content of the ideas of European neo-pagans like Gerard and what makes them so enamored of Hinduism. Are these ideas conducive to a good society which can deliver what modern Indian state is constitutionally obliged to provide: equal rights of citizenship to all, regardless of creed or caste?

The answer, as we shall see, is a resounding No. In his address to Hindu Adhyayan Kendra which is posted on the French New Right website, Gerard tries to establish a kinship with Hindu nationalists by insisting that because India and Europe have "common roots", they also have "common enemies". Who are these enemies out to destroy India and Europe? He lists two, both of which he attributes ultimately to the Judeo-Christian, Semitic-monotheistic ways of thinking, especially (to paraphrase Gerard) as it is showing up in the hordes of Islamic immigrants threatening the civilizations of Europe and India alike.

The two immediate threats Gerard lists are: environmental degra-dation and "humanitarian materialism" of both Marxist and capitalist varieties which preach a "totalitarian egalitarianism" which condemns natural differences like caste, and propagate "freedom" of the individual from his affiliations of race, class, religion and even sex with the exaltation of homosexuality. But, Gerard believes that both of these threats stem from a more fundamental enemy and that is "Semitic monotheism" or "Judeo-Christian thinking" which converts all cultures to a universal, homogenous style of thinking, making them reject their primary affiliations with their own gods, their own tribe and their own land. He believes that all universalist and egalitarian ideas which deny natural distinctions and organic relationships are products of Judeo-Christian way of thinking which seeks to convert everyone and everything to "the single model, be it one God, the single party system or the single market..." The ultimate cause of all the problems of modernity is this Judeo-Christian zeal to convert. He singles out Islam as the most dangerous example of Abrahamic monotheism, claiming that the high rate of immigration and population growth of Muslims is aimed at "universal conquest".

Next in line for condemnation are the Marxists who he declares to be merely "secularized Christians". What he finds objectionable with both Christians and Marxists is this:

> they demonize the old cast [sic] system, which preserved during centuries the identity of India against all exterior aggression. Due to this intellectual terrorism, it is now difficult to tell the truth about casts [sic] which are an important part of India's genius. Authors like Danielou or Dumont dare to say the truth: casts [sic] are inherent in human nature.

We come a full circle to Guru Golwalkar's defense of natural inequality quoted above. The polytheism and paganism Gerard recommends welcomes the inequities of caste which are "inherent in human nature" and created by the working of the spirit in nature. Whatever is natural must be obeyed and worshipped.

All this, by the way, is pure unadulterated philosophy of the French New Right. It is one of the central dogmas of the New Right that all elements of the modern age – individualism, decasualization, rationalization and universalism – are simply secularized versions of Christian metaphysics. Universalism, be it religious or secular, is held responsible for suppressing the natural differences among people, communities and races. The goal of the New Right is to make difference respectable again, to replace the old biological racism of the fascists and old Right with the right to live according to one's own culture and one's own religion, an ideal which goes against the grain of modern civil societies which are constituted by shared secular culture.[8] It is not therefore a mere coincidence that Gerard's love letter to Hinduism ends up with de Benoist's collection: Gerard shares the deepest convictions of the New Right – with the blessing of the elders of Hindu nationalism.

If monotheism is the problem, recovery of polytheism is the obvious solution. This is indeed what is offered: after scoffing at the socialist ideal of each according to his needs, Gerard recommends that we "restore the dharma", which teaches "each according to his traditions", where traditions are understood as "innate essences of different religions and groups". Combine this with the widespread notion in Hindutva circles that Hindus are innately tolerant and respectful of difference, the obvious conclusion is that return to polytheism of Hindus (which is a "cousin" of early Greek and Roman pagans) will save the world.

Why should substituting Abrahamic God with many gods save the world? This is exactly where deep ecology comes in handy. Many gods who inhabit the earth will make nature sacred once again and lead to better care of it. Good environmental citizenship is the public face of paganism and neo-Hinduism. Indeed, racist neo-pagans routinely infilterate non-racsist radical ecology groups by espousing ecological themes.[9] This is the reason why an easy acceptance of dharmic ecology by the left is problematic: it confers respectability on archaic and socially divisive ideas.

7.

But the defenders of religious environmentalism might still ask: So what? Just because the right-wing is opportunistically jumping on to the ecology bandwagon and bringing foreign neo-pagans along, it does not mean that religion cannot be an effective check against environmental degradation.

But by now there is sufficient evidence from anthropological studies that nature worship plays a highly ambiguous role in how people relate to nature. Just because people hold some rivers, trees, stones, animals as sacred do not mean that they do it out of environmental concerns. Wish-fulfillment (e.g., for better rains, higher crop yields), fear, ancestor worship are fairly common motivations for nature worship. Indeed, as the important work by Kelly Alley and Vijaya Nagrajan[10] has shown, those who see the Ganga as a goddess or the earth as a Bhu Devi actually take less care of them: the river and the earth are seen as divine beings and therefore capable of cleansing themselves, as well as cleansing the karma of human devotees. Goddesses do not need the help of mere mortals for their survival. My point is that the underlying assumption of religious environmentalism – that a religious attitude of sacredness and reverence toward nature encourages wise use of nature – is not supported by sound evidence from field studies.

In closing, I would like to return to a hard learned, but mostly forgotten, lesson of the environmental movement in India. The lesson is this: most poor people participate in environmental movements for secular reasons. In study after study, it has come to light that the primary motivation of the poor people to take action on behalf of the trees, rivers and land is their interest in a better life materially for themselves and for their children. The poor are no where as technology averse, as their urban middle class activist "consciousness-raisers" are. Most of the time, they are fighting to get a better deal out of development projects, not to stop them altogether.

This secular motivation for environmental action is an untapped resource for secular environmentalism. Rather than drape the cloak of sacredness on nature, environmentalism in India can become a source of secularism and a class-based collective action.

Notes

1 This is a revised text of my talk in the Nature/Religion/Knowledge/Politics Lecture Series, Syracuse University, Nov. 9, 2004.

2 See "India's temple to AIDS goddess", Dec. 2, 1999, BBC News, available at www.news.bbc.co.uk. It boggles the imagination how performing arti before an idol is supposed to encourage awareness regarding AIDS.

3 Personal communication with an IAS officer who was in the US on a study leave and who happened to attend the seminar in Syracuse University where I read this paper.

4 See Vasant Kaiwar (2005) for an illuminating essay on how the Oriental Renaissance in the 19th and early 20th centuries left behind the notion of Hindus as "Aryan" people, either as native to India (as mostly German Orientalists thought) or as outsiders who nevertheless found the fulfillment of their "Aryan" culture in India (as mostly the British Orientalists thought).

5 See the important monographs by Mattias Gardell (2003) and Jeffrey Kaplan (1997). They examine the slow but steady displacement of KKK and Christian Identity ideologies in the Far Right by racist pagan groups who believe America to be the homeland of white Nordic races who "discovered" it before Columbus. Pagan revival of Norse gods and rituals are an important feature of the White Power groups in America.

6 Earth First! an anti-racist deep ecology group had to apologize for running the ad. For details, see Taylor (2002) .

7 See Nouvelle Droite-New Right-English articles at http://foster.20megsfree.com/index_en.htm. This website also has Vandana Shiva among the many contributors.

8 A recent manifesto of the French New Right titled " The French New Right in the Year 2000" can be found on Nouvelle Droite website. See note 6.

9 See the essays collected in Kaplan (1997) and Gardell (2003).

10 Both in Nelson (1998).

References

Adler, Margot. 1986. Drawing Down the Moon. New York: Penguin.

Albanese, Catherine. 2002. Reconsidering Nature Religion. Harrisburg: Trinity Press.

Chapple, Christopher K. and Mary E. Tucker, eds. Hinduism and Ecology: The Intersection of Earth, Sky and Water. Harvard University Press.

Chapple, Christopher,K. 1998. Toward an Indigenous Indian Environmentalism. In Purifying the Body of God: Religion and Ecology in Hindu India, edited by

Lance E. Nelson, Albany: SUNY Press.

Freeman, J.R. 1999. Gods, Groves and the culture of Nature in Kerela. Modern Asian Studies. 33(2): 257-302.

Gardell, Mattias. 2003. Gods of the Blood: The Pagan Revival and White Separatism. Durham, N.C.: Duke University Press.

Golwalkar, Madhav, S. 1966. Bunch of Thoughts. Bangalore: Jagran Prakashan. Available at http://www.hindubooks.org.

Kaiwar, Vasant. 2005. The Aryan Model of History and the Oriental Renaissance: The Politics of Identity in an Age of Revolutions, Colonialism and Nationalism. In The Antinomies of Modernity, edited by Vasant Kaiwar and Sucheta Mazumdar, pp. 13-61. Durham, N.C.: Duke University Press.

Kaplan, Jeffery. 1997. Radical Religion in America. Syracuse: Syracuse University Press.

Lal, Vinay. 2000. Too deep for deep ecology: Gandhi and the Ecological Vision of Life. In Hinduism and Ecology: The Intersection of Earth, Sky and Water, edited by Christopher Chapple and Mary E. Tucker.Harvard University Press.

Mawdsley, Emma. 1998. After Chipko: From Environment to Region in Uttaranchal. Journal of Peasant Studies, Vol. 25, 36-54.

Neslon, Lance, ed. 1998. Purifying the Body of God: Religion and Ecology in Hindu India. Albany: SUNY Press.

Rangan, Haripriya. 2000. Of Myths and Movement: Rewriting Chipko into Himalyan History. London: Verso.

Sedgwick, Mark. 2005. Against the Modern World: Traditionalism and the Secret Intellectual History of the Twentieth Century. New York: Oxford University Press.

Sharma, Mukul. 2002. Saffronizing Green. Seminar, No. 516.

Sharma, Mukul. 2001. Nature and Nationalism. Frontline, Vol. 18, February 3-16.

Sinha, Subir, Shubhra Gururani and Brian Greenberg, 1997. The New Traditionalist Discourse of Indian Environmentalism, The Journal of Peasant Studies, 24 (3): 65-99.

Taylor, Bron. 2002. Diggers, Wolves, Ents, Elves and Expanding Universes. In The Cultic Milieu, edited by Jeffrey Kaplan and Helene Low, pp. 26-74. Walnut Creek, CA: Altamira Press.

York, Michael. 1996. New Age and Paganism. In Paganism Today, edited by Graham Harvey and Charlotte Hardman, San Francisco: Thorsons, Harper Collins, pp. 156-165.

MAKING SCIENCE SACRED
How Postmodernism Aids Vedic Science[1]

Introduction

This is a time of great hopes and great challenges for India. The hope that the democratic process can rein in religious fanaticism comes from the electoral defeat of the BJP and likes of Murli Manohar Joshi, the chief engineer of Hinduization of science and education under the BJP rule. The challenge comes from the realization that the overthrow of the BJP does not mean an end of the ideology of Hindutva that the Sangh Parivar succeeded in infusing into India's civil institutions. The defeat of Joshi does not mean the defeat of Joshism.

Clearly, the partisans of secularism in India cannot afford to rest in the afterglow of the last elections. There is a need to continue to engage with the content of Hindutva ideology in order to refute and discredit its core ideas.

One of the main pillars of the contemporary neo-Hinduism and Hindutva ideology is scientism. Hindutva's scientism shows up in the endlessly repeated mantras that "Hinduism is the religion of the future" because it is "essentially a science" and because, as Swami Vivekananda put it, "Of all the scriptures of the world, Vedanta is entirely in harmony with the results that have been attained by modern science." Many secular critics of Hindutva have not realized how central this myth of Vedas-as-science has been to the nationalist assertions of Hinduism's superiority over other religions. What is more, this self-glorifying myth has been widely accepted by educated middle classes, including many scientists themselves.

The situation is not very different from that in America where the proponents of creation science and intelligent design claim the support of scientific evidence for the Genesis story of the Bible. The difference is that in the US there are influential voices from within the mainline liberal churches who are strongly opposed to creationism. Moreover, there are many world-renowned scientists speaking out against the Christian fundament-alist abuses of science. In India, on the other hand, there are hardly any voices from within the Hindu fold who challenge the myth of Vedic science: nearly the entire religious establishment, from the temple priests to modern gurus and Sanskrit scholars, is united in affirming the "scientific" status of the traditional Hindu worldview. For the most part, Indian scientists have also been complicit in perpetuating the myth of Vedic science. Even those scientists and intellectuals who came out to oppose extreme outrages like Vedic astrology have not taken the time and the trouble to challenge the horrendous distortions of the history and philosophy of modern science which Hindu nationalists use to justify the Vedas as a form of science.

To challenge the conceptions of nature (or matter), knowledge (or truth) and standards of evidence (experiment and logic) that are invoked by the apologists of Vedic science is an enormous project. In my recently published book, Prophets Facing Backward, I have made a beginning.[2] Prophets is about how postmodernist attacks on modern science as a form of mental imperialism have created the intellectual space for "alternative sciences" which are supposedly more hospitable to worldview of women, non-Western cultures and all others who have been silenced by the hegemony of modern science. I show in this book that the arguments Hindu nationalists use to defend the scientificity of the Vedas are no different in their logic, substance and meta-politics (or worldview) from the arguments offered by the postmodernists who claim to speak for progressive causes. It is a matter of great concern that perfectly well-meaning intellectuals who identify deeply with progressive causes of social justice, anti-imperialism, women's rights and sustainable development, have themselves led the way for re-enchantment or re-sacralization of science. As I will show in this essay, many of their arguments find a hospitable home in the Hindutva arguments for "Vedic sciences". Indeed, it is difficult to avoid the impression that postmodernist and multiculturalist critics of modern science have been re-discovering and restating the logic of analogies and equivalences that Hinduism has always used to deny all contradictions and save its fundamental axioms from critical examination. Postmodernists are truly Manu's children.

The argument I am going to present here is complex. I will start with a quick review of Vedic science under BJP. I will move on to define what I mean by postmodernism and why Indian intellectuals were drawn to it. Next, I will ask why religious fundamentalists in all faiths are so obsessed with modern science. I will take a closer look at the peculiar strategy of hierarchical inclusivism by which Hinduism has always co-opted all challenges to the orthodoxy. I will compare Manu, the 2nd century Hindu law-giver with St Augustine, the 4th century Christian theologian in order to highlight this strategy of inclusivism. I will argue that the much celebrated "tolerance" of Hinduism has come at a great price of retarding the growth of science in India. Finally, I will connect the dots between inclusivism of contemporary Hindu nationalists and the relativist philosophies of science.

Hindutva's Doublespeak of Vedic Science

George Orwell can be a useful guide for understanding how modern science gets equated with, or becomes interchangeable with the amorphous grab-bag of Hindu myths, mysticism and philosophy, lumped together as "the Vedas". Indeed, Orwell's doublethink bears an uncanny resemblance with the well-known Hindu tendency to eclectically combine contradictory ideas by declaring them to be simply different names of the "same thing".

Recall how double-think worked in George Orwell's 1984. Words came to mean their opposites: war meant peace, freedom was slavery, and ignorance strength. History was endlessly revised to make the present look like a confirmation of eternal, unchanging truths. Words, representations, facts ceased to mean what they appear to be saying. Shorn of any definite and contestable meanings, words began to be used interchangeably, hybridized endlessly, without any fear of contradictions.

Under the BJP rule, superstitions started getting described as science. Murli Manohar Joshi and his RSS brethren started invoking science in just about every speech and policy statement. But while they uttered the word "science" – which in today's world is understood as modern science – they meant astrology, or vastu, or Vedic creationism, or transcendental meditation or ancient humoral theory of disease taught by Ayurveda, and so on. This was not just talk: state universities and colleges got big grants from the government to offer post-graduate degrees, including PhDs in astrology; research in vastu shastra, meditation, faith-healing, cow-urine and priest-craft was promoted with substantial injections of public money. Nearly every important discovery of modern science was read back into Hindu sacred books: explosion of nuclear energy became the awesome appearance of God in the Bhagavat Gita, the indeterminacy at quantum level served as confirmation of Vedanta, atomic charges became equivalent of negative, positive and neutral gunas, or moral qualities, the reliance of experience and reason in science became the same thing as reliance on mystical experience and so on. Contemporary theories of physics, evolution and biology were willfully distorted to make it look as if all of modern science was converging to affirm the New Age, mind-over-matter cosmology that follows from Vedantic monism. “Evidence” from fringe sciences was used to support of all kinds of superstitions, from Vastu, astrology, “quantum healing” to the latest theory of Vedic creationism. Science and “Vedas” were treated as homologues, as just different names of the same thing. Orwell’s Big Brother would’ve felt right at home!

Another sign of doublespeak was this: On the one hand, BJP and its allies presented themselves as great champions of science, as long as it could be absorbed into “the Vedas”, of course. But on the other hand, they aggre-ssively condemned the secular and naturalistic worldview of science – the disenchantment of nature – as “reductionist”, as “lower knowledge of mere matter,” and “Western” or even “Semitic”. Science yes, and technology yes, but a rational-materialist critique of Vedic idealism no – that became the mantra of Hindutva. (In the Prophets, I have described Hindutva’s zeal to adopt the vocabulary of science and the instrumental reason of technology while rejecting the Enlightenment rationality as “reactionary modernism”.)

Why this over-eagerness to claim the support of science? There is, undoubtedly, a modernizing impulse in all religions, that is, all religions display a desire to make the supposedly timeless truths of theology accept-able to the modern minds raised on a scientific sensibility. “Scientific creationism” among Christians, which is now becoming popular with Islamic fundamentalists as well (see Edis, 2003), is an example of this impulse. But while Christian fundamentalists in America indulge in creationism primarily to get past the First Amendment,[3] Hinduization of science in India is motivated by a deeply chauvinistic nationalism. As originally formulated by Swami Vivekananda, followed up by Sri Aurobindo and repeated endlessly in the far-right tracts of Guru Golwalkar and Savitri Devi, the urge to claim the support of modern science for the Vedas is motivated by the Hindu nationalist urge to declare Hinduism’s superiority as the religion of reason and natural law over Christianity and Islam, which are declared to be irrational and faith-based "creeds". Contemporary Hindu nationalists are carrying on with the neo-Hindu tradition of proclaiming Hinduism as the universal religion of the future because of its superior "holistic science" (as compared to the "reductionist science" of the West). Besides, it is easier to sell traditions and rituals, especially to urban, upwardly mobile men, if they have the blessings of English-speaking "scientific" gurus.

Postmodernism and the Deconstruction of Science

This business of Vedic science has, of course, been going on before anyone had ever heard the word "postmodern". But – and this is central to my thesis – this Hindu nationalist appropriation of science has found new sources of intellectual respectability from the postmodernist, anti-Enlightenment turn taken by intellectuals, most radically in American universities, but also in India. (Indeed, intellectuals of Indian origin made original contributions to postcolonial theory).[4] Many of the arguments for "decolonizing know-ledge", and constructing "holistic sciences" in tune with the Indic civilizational values converge with the arguments used by the Hindu nationalists. But that is not the worst of it. As they condemned modern science and the Enlightenment rationality ("scientific temper" as it used to be called in India), Indian intellectuals championed the use of un-reformed religious traditions for indigenist versions of science, development, environmentalism, feminism and other causes dear to progressive social movements. Their uncritical embrace of traditions from the populist, third-positionist, mostly neo-Gandhian perspective, left very little space for a principled opposition to the rapid Hinduization of the public sphere. Indeed, many of these new social movements (Chipko, patriotic science movement and elements of anti-globalization movement, for example) have become indistinguishable from similar initiatives from the right.

What do I mean by postmodernism and how did it play out in

India? Postmodernism encompasses a wide variety of theoretical discourses, touching on everything from literature and history to architecture. What unites them is a suspicion of all forms of universal knowledge which claim to represent the world objectively and transparently. Modern natural science, being the ideal-type of such knowledge, naturally became a target of postmodernist critics. In what follows, I will present a very brief account of the postmodern turn in "science studies", a new- fangled discipline devoted to deconstructing modern science, which in turn, became the target of deconstruction by Alan Sokal, the physicist who revealed its inanities in his well-known hoax.[5]

Before it became a candidate for deconstruction, modern natural science was held up as a model of universal discourse. It was widely accepted that while there could be different styles in art, literature, mythology, culinary tastes and the like, there is only one science, and that the criteria of justification of scientific inquiry cut across national and cultural differences. Following the pioneering work of Joseph Needham, it was accepted that while all societies have their own ethno-sciences in the past, these are only tributaries that flow into the ocean of modern scientific knowledge. What makes modern science universal is that it has progressively learned how to learn better, or how to correct itself through socially institutionalized ways of subjecting existing knowledge to empirical tests. Because of its cumulative nature, ethno-sciences of all cultures have to test their theories against what has been learned about nature through the developments in modern science. Sure, there were many critics of this universal science, including prominent scientists themselves, but their criticisms were leveled at the abuses of science, not at its logic.

With postmodernism, this ecumenical, universalistic view of science comes to an end. Mistrust of science's claims to objective, value-free facts began to gather force around the time of Vietnam War and civil rights struggles in the West and around the time of

Emergency in India. Deep disillusionment with the military-industrial complex in the West and the top-down model of development in India were the major engines of a radical critique which decried not just abuses of science, but its very claims to objectivity and universality. In India, modern science came under fire from well-known public intellectuals like Ashis Nandy, Vandana Shiva, Shiv Vishvanathan, Claude Alvares and others associated with the Center for Study of Developing Societies in Delhi and with the emerging ecology and alternative technology movements around the country. These critics condemned modern science as being innately barbaric, violent and even genocidal because of its "reductionism" and its imposition of Western interests and values in collusion with Westernized Indian elite. One can debate the strengths and weaknesses of the Nehruvian model of moderni-zation. But a definite stream in the critiques of science and technology that emerged at this time was not limited to uses or abuses of science: it questioned the content and methodology of science as we know it.

The Indian critique of science found its theoretical justification in theories of social constructivism, also called the Strong Program in socio-logy of science, that claimed to follow Thomas Kuhn's work (even though Kuhn repudiated them). The Strong Program, put forward by David Bloor and Barry Barnes from the University of Edinburgh, claimed that not just the agenda, but the very content of natural science were socially constructed. In their view, all knowledge, regardless of whether it is true or false, rational or irrational, whether it is modern science or traditional knowledge of non-modern cultures is equally conventional or perspectival. In all cases, it is the social interests and cultural and religious meanings, metaphors and metaphysical assumptions that decided how the natural world will be classified, what kind of observations will be accepted as legitimate evidence and what kind of logic will be accepted as reasonable.

No one can deny that there are alternative, culture-dependent descrip-tions of nature: the world is full of a vast variety of such descriptions. Given this diversity, can we not say that modern science provides us a closer, a more approximate representation of nature which is more adequately supported by evidence and logic? Not so, according to social constructivists, because the standards of truth and falsity are also relative to the "form of life" of a culture. To quote Barry Barnes and David Bloor, "the labels 'true' and 'false' are simply different names for cultural preferences". The grand conclusion of this school of thought is that all ways of knowing are at par because all are culturally embedded attempts to understand brute reality. There is only one reality, different cultures approach it differently, each of which is rational in its own context. (If you replace culture with "castes", or "creeds" in this statement, you get the golden rule of Hinduism that all paths to truth are different only in name. But more on this in the next two sections).

Social constructivists do not deny that modern science has discovered some truths about nature that are universally valid – Newton's law of gravity, for example. But even these universals are seen as products of the Judeo-Christian and masculine assumptions of Western cultures. To paraphrase Sandra Harding, one of the best known proponents of feminist standpoint epistemology, other cultures are capable of producing alternative universals of their own. Which culture's "universals" get universalized and which ones are consigned to the status of ethno-sciences is not decided by superior explanatory power, but by superior political power. Well-known scholars, including Andrew Ross and David Hess, wrote books arguing that the line between accepted science and heterodox sciences of cultural minorities is an arbitrary construct reflecting cultural and ideological interests of those in power. Dipesh Chakrabarty, a subaltern historian, expressed the sentiment well when he wrote that "reason (capital R) is but a dialect backed by an army".

To "provincialize Europe", and to present India as source of alternative universals that could heal the logocentrism and dualism of Western science, emerged as the major preoccupation of Indian followers of science studies. Vandana Shiva wrote glowingly of Indian views of non-dualism as superior to Western reductionism. Ashis Nandy embraced this post-Kuhnian paradigm and declared astrology to be the science of the poor and the non-Westernized masses in India. Prayers to smallpox goddess, menstrual taboos, Hindu nature ethics which derive from orthodox ideas about prakriti or shakti, and even the varna order were defended as rational (even superior) solutions to the cultural and ecological crises of modernity.

All this fitted in very well with Western feminist and deep-ecologists' search for a kinder and gentler science that could undo the dualisms or "logocentrism" of modern science. Prominent feminist theorists (led by Carolyn Merchant and Evelyn Keller) condemned the separation of the subject from the object as a sign of masculine thinking. History of modern science was rewritten to decry the progressive secularization or disenchant-ment of nature as a source of oppression of nature and of women. This naturally created an opening for Eastern cultures, especially India, where such secularization of nature is frowned upon by religious doctrines and cultural mores. In the recent literature on Hindu ecology, the most orthodox philosophies of Hinduism, including Advaita Vedanta, vitalistic ideas of life-force (shakti, Brahman) embodied in all species through the mechanism of karma and rebirth, began to be presented as more conducive to feminist and ecological politics. The deep investment of these philosophies in perpetuating superstitions and patriarchy in India was forgotten and forgiven (see Chapter 2 for more details).

The critics went further: They argued that if, in the final analysis, all representations of nature are cultural constructions, then different cultures and subcultures should be permitted to construct their own representations of nature. To judge other cultures from the vantage point of modern science, as the Enlightenment tradition demanded, amounted to an act of "epistemic violence" against the other, as Gayatri Spivak called it. This became the foundation of what is called postcolonial theory, which combined a perspectival epistemology with Michel Foucault's notion of power of discourse and Edward Said's theory of Orientalism. Postcolonial theory led to a flood of discourse analyses showing how the modernist critics of tradition – especially Nehru, but also the nationalist neo-Hindus like Bankim Chandra, Rammohun Roy and other leading lights of the Indian Renaissance – were mentally colonized because they were seeing India through Western conceptual categories. Any change that challenged India's "unique cultural gestalt", as Nandy liked to call it, was to be resisted.

All told, preservation of cultural meanings took priority over validity. Objectively false cosmology of the "other" was not to be challenged because it gave meaning to people's lives. Any demand for self-correction of local knowledges was routinely decried as a rationalist "witch-hunt". The alternative to Needhamian universalism was that of "critical traditionalism" or "borderland epistemologies". Like a bricolage, pastiche or a cyborg, cultures should be encouraged to create an eclectic mix of different and even contradictory ways of knowing. One need not reject modern science altogether, but rather selectively absorb it into the Indian gestalt: this was the message of the so-called "critical traditionalism" that postcolonial thinkers like Ashis Nandy and Bhiku Parekh derived from Gandhi. Contra-dictions were not to be questioned and removed, but rather celebrated as expressions of difference.

Religious Fundamentalists and Science

The important thing to understand about religious fundamentalism is that it is an ideology of a 'closed society'. Closed societies, if you follow Karl Popper, are societies that do not allow any rational criticism or falsification of their fundamental moral laws, which they treat as having the backing of inevitable laws of nature put in place by God. As past experience shows, closed societies are not anti-scientific. On the contrary, they are hyper-scientistic, that is, they claim the support of existing science for their dogmas, and in turn use these dogmas to constrain scientific research (for example, Lysenkoism in the old USSR).

Fundamentalists are no different. On the one hand, they loudly demonize science when it is used by rationalists to challenge religious myths and superstitions. But on the other hand, they want to lay claims on modern science as being on their side, as affirming their god-centered cosmology and the moral and social norms that follow from that cosmology.

Why this eagerness to the backing of science? Clearly the idea is to evade refutation, deny the obvious contradictions and take on the cultural authority of science for their teleological reading of nature as exhibiting a moral order. As I mentioned earlier, in the case of Hindu nationalism, the urge to prove the superiority of Hinduism over other faiths is an additional factor.

This hyper-scientism is a phenomenon of modern age. In the pre-modern era, science needed the support and consent of theology in order to appear trustworthy and reasonable. In our time, it is the other way around: it is theology that needs the support of science in order to appear trustworthy and rational. No one, except extreme fanatics like the Taliban perhaps, can afford to just say no to modern science, especially at a time when they are all using technologies from the Internet to the nuclear bombs.

So, all fundamentalists want to and try to use modern science as affirming their particular worldview. There are two ways to go about doing it: either by exclusiveness which tends toward literalism, or by inclusiveness, which tends toward relativism, hybridity and an Orwellian doublespeak.

Exclusiveness is the preferred method of Christian and Islamic conservatives: They treat their sacred books as the only truth, valid for all people, for all times. Historically, these traditions have tended to judge other ways of seeing – including, of course, empirical sciences – against the Revealed word of God, and not considered valid within their own contexts. Christianity has developed many ways to deal with the contradictions posed by development of science, from the Copernican theory to Darwinism. Contrary to the impression left behind by creationists, literalist defense of the Bible is not the dominant tendency. From very early on, Christianity has allowed reinterpretation of church dogmas when conflicts arise with well established sciences (see the next section).

Inclusiveness is the preferred method of Hinduism. What makes Hinduism an inclusive religion?

It is not that Hindus do not have their exclusive truths which they consider eternally and universally true: they obviously do. Belief in Brahman as the sole ultimate reality, belief in karma and rebirth, hope for nirvana are all central dogmas of Hinduism – they constitute the hard core of the faith that has survived through many centuries of change. It is not a lack of exclusive dogmas, but a stance of relativism and eclecticism that makes Hinduism inclusive. For example, while the goal of liberation from the endless cycles of birth and rebirth by realizing the Brahman within you is preached as mandatory for all Hindus, the means of achieving the goal are left open, to be decided by the innate capacities, tastes and inclinations of different people, born in different castes, different social contexts and even different countries. As Vivekananda put it, "the absolute can be realized, or thought of, or stated only through the relative…" (This, incidentally, is exactly the position of cultural studies of science: universal natural rationality is not denied, but expressed in so many forms).

But in Hinduism, relativism does not follow from a radical extension of the liberal doctrine of the individual's right to his/her own cultural meanings, as it does in postmodernism. Rather, relativism in Hinduism is a logical corollary of its presumption of innate inequality of human beings. If Hinduism does not prescribe the same level of access to the same means of salvation to all, it is because it does not treat all persons as equal in abilities, aspirations and needs. If Hinduism does not impose one single truth on all, it is because it does not believe all people are capable of grasping that truth. Hindu relativism is hierarchical in another significant way: while each person/group is left to his/her means of achieving salvation, these means are not considered equal in value. The Gnostic knowledge of the nirguna Brahman within is considered the pinnacle of all wisdom, while the lower orders are allowed to have their saguna God appear to them in idols or in elements of nature. While the mystical apprehension of Brahman is considered the absolute and the most complete truth of the totality, "lower" knowledges are not rejected as false: they are only "lower" because while true within their own context, they are seen as incomplete and partial.

The flip side of this hierarchical relativism is encompassment. If all ways of knowing or achieving salvation are merely partial and context-bound expressions of the same aspiration, namely, to know reality of Brahman, then, they can be encompassed or accommodated as lower expressions of the Absolute Truth, differing only in their level of reality, or level of complexity and in their choice of words. Because all ways of knowing are trying, in their own limited ways, to get the view of the totality accessible only to Vedanta, they can't really contradict it. The criterion here is not truth or falsity, but hierarchical levels of truth, with the "higher" (read: spiritual and mystical knowledge) simply treating the "lower" (read: material and sensory knowledge) as an imperfect, incomplete versions of itself. The possibility that the "lower" may actually expose the "higher" as an empty illusion is simply not entertained. Thus while Hinduism appears more non-judgmental and tolerant, it does not treat other ways of knowing as potential competitors and equals which can actually falsify the eternal truths of Vedanta. The inclusiveness of Hinduism is a mask of its hubris and self-aggrandization.

Hindu Inclusiveness and its Impact on Growth of Science

I want to take a quick look at how Hindu inclusivism co-evolved with the logic of caste in India and how it prevented the growth of critical reason.

By the time Manu wrote his Manusmriti, the Upanishads had been written, Varna or caste system had been consolidated and the battle between Brahmins and the assorted heretics who denied the authority of the Vedas was going on. The situation in India was not very different from Greece at the time of Plato's academy – like the pre-Socratic materialists, we had our materialist philosophers, the Lokayata, charvakas and samkhya; like Socrates, we had the Buddha who emphasized critical reason. All of them were locked in an ideological battle with the Brahmins over the nature of the ultimate reality and how we can know it. Brahmins insisted that the ultimate reality was spiritual, a disembodied subtle force, quite like Plato's Forms, that pervades nature and animates it. Like Plato's philosophers who could step out of the cave and see the Forms, only those who could discipline the mind through yoga and other meditative practices could actually see Brahman on their mind's eye. The non-Vedic sects denied that the ultimate reality was made of spirit: Buddha denied the existence of atman, Lokayata were strict materialists, as were early Samkhyas who believed in the self-sufficiency of nature.

What was going on in Christianity? By the time St. Augustine wrote his major works, Christianity was already the official religion of Rome and the process of Christianizing the pagans was in full swing.

What is of interest to us is the difference between how the two emerging faiths dealt with the materialists.

First thing to note are the amazing similarities. Both Manu and St. Augustine insist that reason and secular knowledge accessible to human senses must serve as a handmaiden to theology: knowledge of natural phenomena could only affirm the truths of the Vedas or the Bible, but never question it.

Let us look at St. Augustine first. Augustine grew up as a pagan and was well-educated in Greek classics. He converted to Christianity later in his life. It is very clear that Augustine does not have much use for natural sciences of the Romans or the Greeks. He condemns curiosity as a sin and wants all pagan knowledge to serve Christian ends. But here is the essential difference: when he finds that Greek sciences, especially the science of Aristotle, contradict the creation story in the Genesis, he was perfectly willing to revise the Genesis. Augustine asserts that if there is conflict between a literal reading of the scriptures and a well-established truth about nature, we must seek a metaphorical interpretation of the scripture. The important thing to note is that Augustine treats the pagans as potential partners in a discourse: even though he thinks they are heretics, he does not treat them as outside the fraternity of reason and allows that they could be right and the Christians could be wrong. There is a presumption of the rational unity of mankind – all human beings, being made in God's image, can talk to each other, and are capable of grasping the same level of truth through reason that all are endowed with. Of course, we know the later history of Christianity was hardly kind to pagans and other non-Christians. But Augustine did set the tone that allowed for a revision in Church dogma in the face of contradictory evidence. In fact, Galileo called upon Augustine's authority in his own struggles with the Catholic Church.[6]

Let us go back to Manu. He is equally vehement against the heretics, but he lacks Augustine's belief in the rational unity of mankind: the idea that the heretics could be right and that the Brahmins had something to learn from them just does not occur in Manu or in the subsequent law books. There are passages in Manusmriti where Manu condemns all non-Vedic doctrines as evil, dark and bringers of bad karma (12.95). He does make small concessions here and there: he allows that you can use reason, as long as it does not challenge the Vedas (12: 106). But when it comes to the status of heretics, he is uncompromising: he equates them repeatedly with lower castes, with impure people and even with animals including cats and – for some strange reasons – herons. Even in later more popular religious texts like the Mahabharata and Ramayana, materialists and rationalists are treated as jackals and chandals. In this cosmology, the difference between different groups of human beings is of the same order as difference between distinct species: they are ontologically different, different in the very subs-tance of which they are made, and different therefore in their abilities and needs. How is one to even imagine a mutual conversation, a give-and-take of ideas, from those who you think belong to an inferior order of being from your self? Hierarchy was not just a sociological principle of Hinduism, but also an epistemological principle; it has done as much harm to the growth of science, as to the growth of a decent, egalitarian society in India.

The hierarchical relativism that led to inclusivism was a result of this caste logic: heretics were not considered partners in a mutual dialogue. However much the Christian fathers oppressed the pagans, they considered them worthy and capable of accepting the Biblical truth that they themselves accepted. Brahmins, on the other hand, felt no compulsion to bring who they considered the lower orders into their own fold, either through persuasion, conversion or violence. The knowledge of the Vedas was considered too special and too pure to be handed out to the lower orders. If you don't want to share your gods and your books with others, you can't possibly deny them their gods and their books. The "tolerance" toward others was a product of Brahmins' supreme sense of superiority and arrogance.

But non-Brahmin castes and non-Vedic sects were not left free to develop their own worldviews and practice. Their gods and their rituals and their cosmologies remained subordinated to the knowledge of the Vedas. Due to the control of rituals, which gave them enormous power, the Brahmi-nical ideals of mystical, non-sensory knowledge of Brahman remained the gold standard of truth and knowledge. All others were seen as limited and inferior paths to the knowledge of Brahman: they were true as partial, inferior attempts to get to the ultimate knowledge accessible only to those who know the Vedas. In order to get any hearing at all, non-Vedic thinkers had to show that their ideas did not contradict the Vedas and that their goal was essentially the same as prescribed by the Vedas. This is not my own idiosyncratic reading. Let me quote from Surendranath Dasgupta, one of the most regarded sympathetic exponents of Hindu philosophy:

> It was almost universally believed by the Hindus [that] the highest truths could only be found in the revelations of the Vedas…the highest knowledge of the ultimate truth and reality was regarded as having been once and for all, declared in the Upanishads…it was therefore thought to be extremely audacious that any person, howsoever brilliant and learned he might be, should have any right to say anything regarding the highest truth simply on the authority of his own opinion and reasons…
>
> … In order to make himself heard, it was necessary for him to show that the texts of the Upanishads supported him and that their purport was the same…. Such was the high esteem and respect for [the Vedantic sutras] that whenever the later writers had any new speculations to offer, these were reconciled with the doctrines of one or the other of the existing systems and put down as faithful interpretation of the system…all independence of thought was limited and enchained by the faith of the school to which they were attached. Instead of producing a succession of free-lance thinkers having their own systems to propound, India brought forth schools of pupils who carried the traditionary views of a particular system from generation to generation... and reconciled the new solutions with the older teachings without ever contradicting them (Dasgupta, 1922: 41, 63, 66, emphases added).

In other words, the "eternal truths" of the Vedas were literally unquestionable. They were shielded from refutations by subsuming the new into the old, by turning innovations into derivatives of eternal traditions. Hinduism universalized itself not by violence against the bodies of those who disagreed with its holy truths, but by doing violence to their ideas. The heretics, or "Veda-virodhi" as Shankara called them, were allowed to live, but their ideas were turned into mere copies of all that was already contained in the Vedas. Sociologically, this violence was made possible by the exclusive access to the so-called magic and rituals that Brahmins had. Philosophically, this violence was done by declaring unlike ideas to be like, or by claiming equivalences, homologies or resemblance between new ideas and the teachings of the Vedas. As Brian Smith (1989: 46-49) has argued so cogently, establishing resemblances or likenesses between fundamentally unlike and even contradictory ideas is the central episteme of Vedic orthodoxy. Hinduism does not judge the validity of ideas by the force of independently testable evidence warranting them, but by their degree of resemblance with the Vedic prototype.[7] Just as sociologically higher castes encompass those lower, philosophically, the higher spiritual truths of Vedanta are supposed to encompass and contain all empirical truths, including the truths of modern science.

Take away all the layers of sophistry and you will discover that the ultimate logic that justifies this Hindu episteme of hierarchical resemblances is nothing more than radical contextualism, not very different from social constructivism described above. Different paths (marga), doctrines (mata) and traditions (sampradaya) can be treated as exchangeable synonyms of Vedas because all are supposed to be rational within their own contexts. Other doctrines and ways of knowing, in other words, are seen as aspiring for truth as much as the Vedas are, but they are limited by their limited contexts. Vedas are superior because they apply the rational quest of knowledge to all of existence, including the spiritual realms not accessible through ordinary senses. (The question how do we know if this spiritual realm exists if we cannot access it through ordinary senses has never been convincingly answered by Hindu apologists). Because all are essentially rational, they can be treated as synonyms and used interchangeably without worrying about contradictions. This means that the achievements of other knowledge systems become achievements, ultimately, of the Vedas, because all ways of knowing are contained in it. It also means that nothing can contradict the Vedas because the truth or falsity of other knowledge systems are decided by their own limited contexts.

This episteme of resemblances and equivalences has been the bane of rational thought throughout India's history. There is ample evidence that even the most learned astronomers like Brahmagupta had to suppress their naturalistic understanding of eclipses in favor of superstitions about demons eating up the sun or the moon; physicians in the Ayurvedic tradition had to make concessions to atman and karma when they actually had a naturalistic theory of disease.[8] The end result was that natural philosophy was not totally absent, but it remained subordinated to the higher truths of the spirit.

Not surprisingly, when the thinkers of the so-called Hindu renaissance,[9] encountered modern science brought in by the British, they took this upper-caste inclusivist stance toward it: they did not deny the importance of modern science, but declared it to be an inferior and limited kind of knowledge which only gave us knowledge of "mere matter" which needed to be taken to a "higher" or mystical level where matter becomes one with consciousness, the subject merges with the object. Whereas in the West, where contradictions with truth were taken seriously, developments of natural science had led to a questioning of the existence of "higher" realms, in Hinduism, science was relegated to its own limited and lower order of things. In keeping with the cultural habits of Hinduism, neo-Hindu thinkers like Rammohun Roy, Vivekananda, Aurobindo and Radhakrishnan all denied any need to revise the essentials of Brahminical idealism which treats matter as an illusion created by the spirit. They simply fitted science in the hierarchical scheme, with spiritual knowledge – capital-T Truth of the mystics – at the top. There were rationalist voices in the margins of the Indian society, confined to the leadership of Ambedkarite neo-Buddhist dalits, the atheistic leadership of Periyar's self-respect movement, and the philosophical materialists among the Marxists, socialists and radical humanists. But these voices failed to displace the hegemony of Hindu ideals of spiritual knowledge as the highest knowledge.

If the essence of the Enlightenment lies in establishing new empirical criteria for judging the validity of knowledge, then one can safely say that the Enlightenment bypassed India. The Brahminical conception of Absolute Truth which cannot be accessed by "mere" senses but can only be "directly realized" through intuition or "supra-rational experience" (to use S. Radharkrishnan's vocabulary) remained the ideal of superior knowledge. Developments in technology, industry and economy have not resulted in revision in ways of thinking in the social and cultural realm. The ease with which Hindutva could gain the intellectual allegiance of the educated middle classes, many of them with advanced degrees in sciences, is a result of the historic failure of the Indian Enlightenment.

Postmodernism as the Philosophy of Inclusivism

It is my contention that the picture of science that social constructivism offers is tailor-made for the doublespeak that results from the hierarchical inclusivism so characteristic of traditional Hinduism. Social constructivism provides a new logic for the age-old Hindu episteme of denying contradic-tions by establishing likenesses between unlike ideas, or resemblances between modern science and "alternative ways of knowing". If all ways of knowing are equally socially constructed, then they are at par and one cannot contradict, or challenge, the other. All sciences become equivalent and therefore, interchangeable. The old idea of a rational critique of metaphysics in the light of empirically warranted knowledge goes out of the window. All the major conclusions of science studies – culturally different but equally rational paths to truth, equation of universalism with colonialism and totalitarianism, penchant for eclecticism and hybridity, and the condemnation of disenchantment of nature – end up restating the fundamental assumptions which the nationalist neo-Hindus have always used to assert the superior "scientificity" of Hindu metaphysics and mysticism. Postmodern prophets who promise us a kinder, gentler science do indeed face backward to the spirit-soaked metaphysics of orthodox Hinduism, which has, in fact, inhibited the growth of reason, equality and freedom in India.

Unlike the Abrahamic religions which are weary of epistemological relativism out of the fear of relativizing the Word of God revealed in the Bible or the Koran, Brahminical Hinduism (and Hindu nationalism) thrives on a hierarchical relativism to evade all challenges to its idealistic meta-physics and mystical ways of knowing. Rather than accept the naturalistic and empirical theories of modern science as contradicting the Vedantic philosophy – which they actually do – Hindu nationalists simply declare modern science to be true only within its limited materialistic assumptions. They do not reject modern science (who can?) but "merely" treat it as one among the many different paths to the ultimate truth, which is known only to the Vedic Hinduism.

In theory, of course, social constructivists deny the very possibility of truth and that does differentiate them from religious zealots of all faiths who want to hold on to the literal truth of their creeds. But since in practice, it is not easy to live without some notion of truth – not even social constructivists live without accepting some statements as true – it is the relativist aspects of postmodernist social theory that actually percolate down into the cultural space. By treating truth in proportion to the evidence for it, modern science in fact provides the only sensible alternative to the religious notion of "ultimate truth". But by venting their fury on science and insisting on the ideological nature of scientific objectivity, post-modernists have left no middle ground between the ultimate truths of religions and the relativist truths of cultures. Hindu nationalist genius has been to use the relativist view of truth to protect the Hindu conception of ultimate truth from any challenge. By enshrining relativism as a source of empowerment of the weak, social constructivist theory has unintentionally provided intellectual respectability to the strategy of hierarchical inclusivism which is the time-tested method of Hindu apologetics.

Let me, very briefly, give some examples of this convergence between supposedly "emancipatory" postmodernist deconstruction of science and the clearly reactionary, chauvinistic doublespeak of Vedic science.

For starters, take the issue of "decolonizing" modern science. As noted above, developing ethno-sciences which comprehend nature through local conceptual categories of women, non-Western people and other cultural minorities has been a cornerstone of social constructivism and postcolonial theory.

Well, Hindu nationalists see themselves as a part and parcel of this postcolonial enterprise. They justify developing a science in accord with the Vedic cosmology as an attempt to decolonize the "Hindu mind" of Western, Semitic-monotheistic influences introduced by Macaulay and Marx. Indeed, scholars-activists sympathetic to the Hindu worldview, including Rajiv Malhotra and Koenard Elst routinely cite the writings of Ashis Nandy, Ronald Inden and even Gayatri Spivak as allies in a shared project of understanding India through Hindu categories.

Like the postmodernist supporters of ethno-sciences, they do not deny that modern science has discovered some truths about nature. But they declare them to be lower-level truths, because they "merely" deal with dead matter, shorn of consciousness. Notwithstanding all pious declarations of the "death" of the Newtonian world view of matter obeying mechanical laws, the fact is that any number of rigorous, double-blind tests have failed to show any signs of disembodied consciousness or mind-stuff in nature: matter obeying mindless laws of physics is all there is. But in the Vedic science discourse, the overwhelming evidence for adequacy of matter to explain the higher functions of mind and life are set aside as a result of "knowledge filtration" by Western-trained scientists.

Take the example of the emerging theory of "Vedic creationism" (which updates the spiritual evolutionary theories of Sri Aurobindo and Swami Vivekananda). Its chief architects, Michael Cremo and Richard Thompson actually cite social constructivist theories to claim that Darwinian evolutionary biologists and mainstream biologists, being products of the Western ontological assumptions, have been systematically ignoring and hiding evidence that supports the theory of "devolution of species" from the Brahman through the mechanism of karma and rebirth. All knowledge, they claim, parroting social constructivism, is a product of interests and biases. On this account, Vedic creationism, explicitly grounded in Vedic cosmology, is as plausible and defensible as Darwinism is on the naturalistic and capitalist assump-tions of the Western scientists.

Vedic creationism is only one example of "decolonized science". More generally, Hindu nationalists from Swami Vivekananda, Deen Dayal Upadhyaya to Murli Manohar Joshi and his brethren in RSS routinely insist on the need to develop a science that is organically related to the innate nature, svabhava or chitti of India. India's chitti, they insist, lies in holistic thought, in keeping matter and spirit, nature and god together (as compared to the "Semitic mind" which separates the two). Like Nandy and other proponents of critical traditionalism and hybridity, Hindu nationalists have been using this purported holism of Hinduism as the touchstone of a uniquely Hindu gestalt: any interpretation of modern science that fits in with this spirit-centered holism is declared to be valid Vedic science while naturalistic, mainstream interpretations are discarded as "Western". The overwhelming enthusiasm for Rupert Sheldrake's occult biology (which builds upon the failed vitalistic theories of Jagdish Chandra Bose) and the near unanimous interpolation of quantum mechanics in mystical terms are examples of the kind of meaning sustaining critical traditionalism and hybridity sanctioned by postmodernists.

But it gets worse. As is well known, Hindu nationalists have been keen on proving that the landmass of India was the original homeland of the "Aryans" and "therefore" the cradle of all civilization. "Vedic Aryans", on this account, were the authors of all natural sciences which, presumably, spread to Greece, Sumeria, China and other major civilizations in antiquity. To substantiate these claims, all kinds of modern scientific discoveries are read back into the Rig Veda, the most ancient of all Vedas. But such boastful claims raise the question of methodology. How did our Vedic forebears figure out the speed of light, the distance between the sun and the earth and why did they code it into the shape and size of fire altars? Similar questions arise for the more general ontological claims that are basic to Hindu metaphysics, namely, there is a higher realm of ultimate reality (Brahman) that cannot be assessed through sensory means. How did our Vedic forbears know it exists and that it actually determines the course of evolution of species, and makes up the gunas of the matter that we all are made of? How can you experience what is beyond all sensory knowledge? But even more important for the claims of scientificity of the Vedas, how do you test the empirical claims based upon that experience?

Here one finds an incredibly brazen claim for relativism and culture-boundedness of rationality. Because in Hinduism there are no ontological distinctions between the spirit and matter, one can understand laws that regulate matter by studying the laws of the spirit. And the laws of spirit can be understood by turning inward, through yoga and meditation leading to mystical experiences. Since all science, supporters of this mysticism-as-science argue, gains its coherence from within its own culturally sanctioned, taken-for-granted assumptions, modern science puts an artificial limit on knowledge as only that knowledge which can be accessible to senses. Within the taken-for-granted assumptions of Hinduism, it is as rational and scientific to take the non-sensory "seeing" – that is mystical and other meditative practices – as empirical evidence of the spiritual and natural realm. This purported scientificity of the non-mechanistic, spiritual realm, in turn, paves the way for declaring occult new age practices like astrology, vastu, and quantum healing and even yagnas as scientific within the Vedic-Hindu universe. This defense of parity (i.e. equal rationality) of the Vedic method of non-sensory, mystical knowing is fundamentally a social constructivist argument: it assumes that all sciences are valid for a given community that shares a fundamental metaphysics.

Over and above these epistemological issues, there is a vast area of agreement over meta-political or worldview issues between postmodernist and Hindu nationalist critics of science. Both see the universal claims of modern science as oppressive and colonial. Both see the disenchantment of nature, the breaking of the bonds between nature and human sense of the sacred as the original sin of the modern era responsible for patriarchy and ecological disasters. Hindu traditionalists share the postmodern rejection of philosophical rationalism, starting with Descartes through Hume and the positivists, as a wrong turn that divests nature of mysteries and turns everything into a matter of quantity. In both cases, the pre-modern tradition is cleansed of its oppressive history and presented as a solution to the problems of the modern age. This is a profoundly reactionary outlook, regardless of whether it comes wrapped in the academic jargon of postmodernism or the shrill chauvinism of Hindu nationalists.

Long ago, Julien Benda wrote in his La Trahison des Clercs, that when intellectuals betray their calling – that is, when intellectuals begin to exalt the particular over the universal, the passions of the multitude over the moral good – then there is nothing left to prevent a society's slide into tribalism and violence. Postmodernism represents a treason of the clerks which has given intellectual respectability to reactionary religiosity.

Notes

1 This is an expanded version of my Daniel Thorner Address at the Masion des Sciences de l'homme, Paris, October 28, 2004. I have added extended quotations

and references to support the basic argument I presented in my talk. Segments of this paper have appeared in the Seminar, No. 545, Annual issue, January, 2005.

2 Prophets Facing Backward: Postmodernism, Science and Hindu Nationalism, New Delhi: Permanent Black. 2004. The American edition appeared earlier, in December 2003, published by Rutgers University Press. For the debate generated by the book, see Nanda (2005).

3 The First Amendment of the US Constitution bars the Congress from making any law that "respects an establishment of religion…" By presenting Biblical creationism as a legitimate science, "creation scientists" are trying to get past the First Amendment bar against teaching religion in public schools. The US courts have consistently denied the scientific credential of creation science.

4 References to the ideas of all those whose names appear in this section can be found in the Prophets.

5 The hoax and some of its aftermath is included in Sokal and Bricmont (1998).

6 This has been argued forcefully by the eminent philosopher of science, Ernan McMullin (1988). See also, Lindberg (2003).

7 A very similar thesis has been put forward more recently by Axel Michaels (2004).

8 See the many writings of Debiprasad Chattopadhyaya. For a good synopsis, see Chattopadhyaya (1976).

9 I am skipping over the Islamic period because I have not – so far – studied the interaction between Islamic and Hindu sciences very well. It is my impression, derived largely from Willhelm Halbfass' writings (1988), that one can find no serious philosophical debate with Islam and Islamic sciences.

References

Chattopadhyaya, Debiprasad. 1976. What is Living and What is Dead in Indian Philosophy. New Delhi: People's Publishing House.

Dasgupta, Surendranath. 1922. A History of Indian Philosophy, Vol 1. New Delhi: Motilal Banarsidass.

Edis, Taner. 2003. A World Designed by God: Science and Creationism in Contemporary Islam. In Science and Religion: Are They Compatible? Edited by Paul Kurtz. Amherst: Prometheus Books.

Halbfass, Wilhelm. 1988. India and Europe: An Essay in Understanding. Albany: SUNY Press.

Lindberg, David. 2003 The Medieval Church Encounters the Classical Tradition: Saint Augustine, Roger Bacon and the Handmaiden Metaphor. In When Science and Christianity Meet. Edited by David C. Lindberg and Ronal L. Numbers, pp. 7-32. Chicago: University of Chicago Press.

McMullin, Ernan. 1988. Natural Science and the Belief in a Creator: Historical Notes. In Physics, Philosophy and Theology: A Common Quest for Understanding. Edited by Robert J. Russell et al., pp. 48-79. The Vatican City State: Vatican Observatory.

Michaels, Axel. 1998. Hinduism: Past and Present. New Jersey: Princeton University Press.

Nanda, Meera. 2005. Response to My Critics. Social Epistemology, Vol. 19, No. 1, pp. 129-73.

Smith, Brian. 1989. Reflections on Resemblance, Ritual and Religion. New York: Oxford University Press.

Sokal, Alan and Jean Bricmont. 1998. Fashionable Nonsense: Postmodern Intellectuals' Abuse of Science. Picador.

www.ingramcontent.com/pod-product-compliance
Lightning Source LLC
LaVergne TN
LVHW011029110826
845149LV00015B/3349

* 9 7 8 8 1 8 8 7 8 9 3 0 6 *